Like an enthusiastic tour guide, Gerald Borchert, a recognized Johannine scholar, leads the reader on a path of history, culture, and literary strategy that illuminates the masterful gospel story with an easily accessible introduction to the narrative. While maintaining an engaging conversational style, he purposely moves us down main highways and back alleys that reveal previously overlooked treasures of insight and inspiration as he draws us deeper and deeper into the gospel's narrative world. *Reading John* is a delightfully unique tour not to be missed!
—Craig McMahan, University Minister and Dean of the Chapel; Director of Mercer on Mission; Assistant Professor in the College of Arts and Sciences, Mercer University

Gerald Borchert's *Reading John* represents a lifetime of faithful scholarship devoted to truth. His observations come from a deep, pastorally sensitive, and lifelong engagement with the text of John in conversation with key scholars. The many ways Borchert elucidates the evangelist's storytelling prowess are impressive and edifying. I know of no other work that so concisely and eloquently explains John's genius and relevance for us today.
—Eric Bolger, Vice President for Academic Affairs and Dean of the College, College of the Ozarks

Gerald Borchert is a skillful guide as he leads readers into the remarkable story world of John's gospel. This work is grounded in solid scholarship and written in an engaging conversational style. The narrative asides, the author's personal experiences, and the interpretive insights provide a fresh rehearing of Jesus' story.
—David May, Landreneau Guillory Chair of Biblical Studies, Central Baptist Theological Seminary

Gerald Borchert is a highly regarded expert on the Gospel of John. Yet, in *Reading John*, he now emerges also as a type of artist who champions the storytelling brilliance of the gospel writer. In fact, this book is written as if Borchert is the "storyteller of the storyteller." It is as if he is speaking his message, surrounded by eager listeners. His remarkable insights and conversational approach make this a book like no other.
—Constance M. Cherry, Professor Emeritus of Christian Worship and Pastoral Ministry, Indiana Wesleyan University

Gerald Borchert's *Reading John* gives readers a new avenue for understanding the gospel. His informal style captures both the amazing simplicity and surprising intricacy of this gospel. He leaves the heavier interpretational matters to the footnotes and focuses instead on drawing the reader into the narrative world of the gospel in the same way that skilled storytellers in every age have engaged their audiences.
—R. Garland Young, Vice President for Academic Affairs; Professor of the Practice of Religion and Greek, Milligan University

Want to read the Gospel of John with fresh eyes? Gerald Borchert writes with enthusiasm and respect for the text, combined with scholarly insights that move beyond superficial observations. He demonstrates how the popular interpretive paradigm of storytelling assists you in understanding John like never before!
—Harry H. Hiller, Director, Cities and Olympics Project; Faculty Professor of Urban Sociology, University of Calgary

Gerald Borchert's *Reading John* continues to reflect the passion, contemporary significance, and scholarly depth that have characterized his work. While the Gospel of John has been seen primarily as a complex theological treatise on the life and teaching of Jesus, Borchert's understanding of this gospel as consisting of a series of interconnected story cycles, artfully constructed by the author, helps the reader hear this gospel through the apostolic storyteller in new, transforming ways.
—Manfred T. Brauch, Former President, Professor Emeritus of Biblical Theology, Palmer Theological Seminary of Eastern University

Gerald Borchert has hit another home run in this fresh approach to reading, reflecting, and meditating on the Gospel of John. The delight that Borchert takes in God's self-revelation in Jesus the Christ, as told by the Johannine storyteller, is truly contagious. We should read this artful work devotionally and fall in love again with God through the Holy Spirit leading the reader to the incarnate Son, whose life, death, and resurrection renew the entirety of creation.
—James R. Hart, President, The Robert E. Webber Institute for Worship Studies

In the beginning was the Word, and the Word became an incarnated Story. Gerald Borchert leads us in reading John's Good News story of Jesus through the captivating lens of ancient oral storytelling. His firm academic footing and faithfulness to the text offer us a clear portrayal of authenticity for our own journey of incarnating the Word in the world of today.
—Ralph Korner, Academic Dean and Professor of Biblical Studies, Taylor Seminary (Canada)

Reading John

The Bible's Transforming Storybook

Gerald L. Borchert

© 2023

Published in the United States by Nurturing Faith Inc., Macon GA,
www.nurturingfaith.net.

Library of Congress Cataloging-in-Publication Data is available.

ISBN: 978-1-63528-220-7

All translations of the biblical texts in this work have been rendered from the Hebrew and Greek texts by the author, although he readily admits his thought processes have been influenced considerably by a combination of the King James and Revised Standard versions of the Bible. The nuances and his understandings, however, are his.

On the Cover: Throughout Christian history the eagle has been associated with the Gospel of John.

This book is gratefully dedicated to students past and present from many countries who have learned with me, as together we have probed the incredible depths of John's gospel stories. Many of those former students are now administrators, professors, ministers, and active lay persons, while some have passed on to meet the Savior of the world.

Webber Institute Books

Webber Institute Books (WIB) serves as the publishing arm of the Robert E. Webber Institute for Worship Studies (IWS). The Institute was founded by the late Robert E. Webber for the purpose of forming servant leaders in worship renewal with the perspective that "the way to the future necessarily runs through the past." IWS is the only school in North America dedicated solely to graduate education in biblical foundations, historical development, theological reflection, and cultural analysis of worship. Its vision emphasizes that its graduates will "participate intentionally in the story of the Triune God" in order to "bring renewal in the local and global church by shaping life and ministry according to that story." In scope it is "gospel-centered in nature and ecumenical in outlook, embracing and serving the whole church in its many expressions and variations." Those interested in obtaining further information concerning the Institute should consult www.iws.edu.

Webber Institute books are published by agreement with Nurturing Faith (www. nurturingfaith.net) to provide a means for disseminating to the general public varying and differing views concerning the many aspects of worship and Christian life. The ideas expressed in these published materials wholly remain the views of the authors themselves and are not necessarily those of IWS or the publisher.

It is the prayerful concern of both IWS and WIB that the information contained in these works will stimulate further reflection and discussion. The results of such exchange of ideas hopefully will enhance worship renewal within the various segments of the Christian church. Moreover, in keeping with the hopes and dreams of founder Bob Webber, may all that is done through this publishing enterprise enable Christians to reject the narcissistic patterns prevalent in contemporary society and give the glory to God who sent Jesus, the Christ, to provide for human transformation and in concert provided humans with the divine triune presence through the Holy Spirit.

Robert Myers　　　　**Gerald L. Borchert**
General Editor　　　　Founding Editor

James Hart
President, IWS

Other Religious/Theological Works by Gerald L. Borchert

Dynamics of Evangelism. Word Books, 1976.

Spiritual Dimensions of Pastoral Care. Westminster, 1985.

Paul and His Interpreters. TSF-IBR (InterVarsity), 1985.

Discovering Thessalonians. Guideposts, 1986.

Assurance and Warning. Broadman, 1986; Word N Works (Singapore), 2006.

The Crisis of Fear. Broadman Press, 1988.

"John" in the Mercer Commentary of the Bible. Mercer University Press, 1995, 1996
    (Translated into Portuguese and Russian).

John 1–11 in the New American Commentary. Broadman & Holman, 1996.

John 12–21 in the New American Commentary. Broadman & Holman, 2002.

"Galatians" in Romans and Galatians in Cornerstone Biblical Commentary. Tyndale House,
    2007 (Translated into Chinese).

Worship in the New Testament: Divine Mystery and Human Response. Chalice, 2008.

"Revelation" in the NLT Study Bible. Tyndale House, 2008, 2017.

Jesus of Nazareth: Background, Witnesses, and Significance. Mercer University Press, 2011.

Assaulted by Grief: Finding God in Broken Places. Mossy Creek/Carson-Newman Press, 2011.

The Lands of the Bible, Vol. 1: Israel, Palestinian Territories, Sinai & Egypt, etc. Mossy Creek/
    Carson-NewmanPress, 2011.

The Lands of the Bible, Vol. 2: In the Footsteps of Paul and John. Mossy Creek/Carson-
    Newman Press, 2012.

Portraits of Jesus for an Age of Biblical Illiteracy. Smyth & Helwys, 2016.

Christ and Chaos: Biblical Keys to Ethical Questions. Nurturing Faith, 2020.

Tension: Empowering Christian Thought and Life. Nurturing Faith, 2021.

Contents

Introduction: The Majesty of Storytelling

Part 1: The Bible's Transforming Storybook
Witness, Believing, and Conflict

Part 2: The Bible's Transforming Storybook
Hour, Farewell, Death, and Resurrection

Preface

As a response to many of my students and to a host of friends, it has been a challenging joy for me to return to analyzing the amazing Gospel of John—this time with a focus on storytelling. This book has been simmering in my mind for many years as I have taught in various parts of the world and written articles and books on various subjects related to the Gospel of John. While I have given attention to many other topics, it is not that I ever left the study of John: this gospel has been foundational for much of my thinking throughout my life.

As I will make clear in the introduction to this work, I have highlighted the fascinating nature of storytelling in the gospel as a prime example and model of early Christian storytelling. While the Johannine stories have come down to us in an exquisitely written theological document, I am convinced that this gospel clearly reflects its roots in the oral culture of the early church. Having published both a longer and shorter commentary and many articles and papers on this gospel, you can understand how this present study grows out of years of reflection.

Accordingly, setting down these subsequent ideas in print has been a refreshing experience for me. Indeed, this work reflects some of the patterns of thinking and teaching by which I have sought to communicate the message of the Johannine gospel to students and lay people for decades. Now in writing this work I have sought to walk the fine line between being sufficiently technical for the scholars (especially in the footnotes) and sufficiently non-technical for interested laypersons and students so that both will find it enticing reading. I have sent this manuscript to various professors and ministers for their views and have asked them to tell me if I have hit the nail on the head in terms of communication, and they have enthusiastically affirmed this work.

I ask you, therefore, to join me in reflecting on how the Johannine storyteller has effectively captured the hearts of countless Christians throughout the centuries. For many followers of Jesus, the Gospel of John has become their favorite book in the Bible. One reason for their attachment to this gospel is that it contains some of the best known and most quoted verses in the Christian canon. But the attachment for Christ-followers to this book goes far beyond quoting favorite biblical proof-texts that may even be painted on posters and exhibited in public gatherings by some well-meaning people who consider that such exhibits are effective means of communicating the gospel.

I would affirm Christians' love of texts such as John 3:16, but I would hope that those devotees of John's gospel would realize that the importance of such a beloved text resides in the contextual framework of a few more verses than just that one in the Nicodemus story. I also hope and pray that the commitment to that story is joined by an even greater zeal, love, and care for others—which is the key to the great command of Jesus in John 13:34-35 and its expansion in 15:12-17.

This work of the Johannine author has certainly been an effective resource for communicating the transforming power of the Son of God who came for a brief period into the world. Indeed, the Johannine storyteller possessed the amazing ability to encapsulate his ideas into vivid stories that lodge in the reader's memory and become epitomized in catch words, phrases, or verses.

For example, the Nicodemus story can be summarized in the popular expression of "born again" (John 3:1-12), or the story of the Samaritan woman can be epitomized in the idea of "not thirst again" (4:13). The experience of Nathaniel meeting Jesus can be linked to the Christianized idea of Jacob's ladder (1:43-51; cf. Gen 28:12), but please remember that neither contemporary humans nor Jacob in those stories ascended and descended on the said heavenly ladder/staircase: that role was given to angels! And, for all who have attended Christian funerals, they are not likely to forget the comfort offered in these consoling words: "Don't let your hearts be troubled" (14:1). And what Christian can forget Jesus' threefold question to Peter, "Do you love me?" that took place around the "second" charcoal fire (21:15-17)?

I trust you will realize that I have always enjoyed teaching these Johannine stories, but it became clear to me—as early as my first year of graduate study—that this gospel is laced with a multitude of themes that are repeated with varying nuances in different stories. So, I quickly learned that one of the best ways to teach students the Gospel of John was to assign them projects that would require them to trace the use of one or more of the Johannine themes throughout this gospel.[1] The responses of my students to such an assignment were overwhelmingly positive because it forced them to see the unifying thought processes that undergird the gospel. But an even more rewarding task is to analyze each of the stories of John and seek to determine how those stories fit into the organization of the Johannine storybook. That concern is the basic reason for this new book.

---

1 See Gerald L. Borchert, *Great Themes From John* (Sioux Falls, SD: North American Baptist Seminary 1966, earlier published by Baptist Life Association News).

Clearly, the Johannine author was an astute storyteller. His language may be quite simple (John's Greek is not complex, as second- and even first-year Greek students can testify), but the importance of his theological ideas can require a great deal more reflection than is normally given to his work.

For example, do not think that a cursory reading of the prologue (1:1-18) will be adequate for understanding those initial eighteen verses. Indeed, they are loaded with implications and theological meaning. The same is true for chapter 2, which contains two very simple yet complex stories with a slightly mystifying conclusion that has not always been adequately interpreted (2:23-25). Similarly, as a former lawyer, I have repeatedly pondered the development of the argument in chapter 5 and how the Johannine storyteller moves Jesus between various roles in his legal confrontation with the Jewish establishment. He knew how to lead his readers into further reflection. And I warn you: do not read chapters 12 and 21 too quickly because you might miss the twists of meaning in the interchanges of those chapters.

My goal here, however, is not to extend this preface or to belabor the significance of themes in John. But let me simply mention a few of those themes so that, as you read this gospel, you will recognize them in the stories. Pay attention to the importance of:

- "light and darkness"
- "truth and lying"
- "seeing and believing"
- "believing and knowing"
- "light and life."

Also give attention to the use of these terms, phrases, and events and their meanings and significance:

- "signs"
- "truly, truly" as an oath
- "the hour"
- "love"
- "judgment"
- "law" (as rules, not as a reflection of God's will)
- "obedience"
- "witness"

- "the lamb of God"
- "king"
- the Jewish festivals (particularly Passover).

Note, also, the contrasts in such concepts as:

- two perspectives of temple
- two resurrections
- two births
- two waters
- two foods
- two meanings for "worship
- "I am" and "I am not" (and who says them).

And it is crucial to understand the centrality of the "Father" and the use of "Son of Man" and "Son of God" in this gospel. These and other themes are embedded in many of the Johannine stories. Be sure you do not miss them!

Now concerning the organization of John, I would remind readers of what most of those who have taken an introductory course of New Testament in college or seminary probably have learned. Briefly stated, while we are not completely certain of the history of our four gospels, it is likely that the Synoptics (Matthew, Mark, and Luke) have resulted from an early borrowing process. We find the basic content of Matthew and Luke to be parallel to Mark, with the addition of sayings or teachings from an unknown source we usually call "Q" (a symbolic designation for the German word "*Quella*," meaning "source") and some additional material in all three gospels that is unique to each one of them.[2] Therefore, much of their content can be found in at least one other of those first three gospels. But such is not true for the Gospel of John. Its organization and content are quite different and therefore appear to be independent of the other three gospels. But something else is also significant, namely: that all the gospels are about Jesus and all report about John the Baptist, and that Jesus…:

---

2 See for example "The Synoptic Problem" in Ralph P. Martin, *New Testament Foundation, Volume 1, The Four Gospels* (Grand Rapids: Eerdmans, 1975, etc.), 139–160.

- …fulfilled the promises of God to the people of Israel.
- …chose twelve or perhaps seven disciples to follow him.
- …healed and fed people.
- …walked on water (the Sea of Galilee/Tiberias).
- …was betrayed by Judas.
- …was rejected by Jewish leadership and the people, and the Jewish leadership arranged for him to be put to death (crucified) by the Roman governor, Pilate.
- …was raised from the dead on the third day and appeared to his disciples, who were instructed to become the primary witnesses of his resurrection and to proclaim the marvelous message of salvation to the world. (Note, however, that the resurrection appearance stories are missing from Mark but are implied there—see Mark 8:31, 9:31, 10:33-34).

But I would pointedly remind you that the presence of these stories in the Gospels represent much of what scholars since C.H. Dodd have defined as the *kerygma*—the foundational elements—of the early church's preaching.[3] Therefore, when one studies the Fourth Gospel, it becomes clear—apart from these kerygmatic elements noted above—that the basic organization of this gospel follows a different pattern than the other gospels.

As a result, you should notice that the Johannine storybook has a different feeling than the other three gospels. That is part of what makes John a unique model of early Christian storytelling. Its stories do not simply give you the factual accounts: they also suggest some of the evangelist's perspectives on those events. Thus, the reader is led by the storyteller to ponder and question what in fact are the implications of each of his selected stories. And one should then consider why several of the stories are different than in the other gospels. (Yes, many of the main stories are quite different! And, yes, those that are similar usually have a particular focus.) So, the storyteller wants the reader (or listener) to probe for the significance or purpose of even the similar stories.

---

3 See C.H, Dodd, *The Apostolic Preaching and Its Development* (London: Hodder & Stoughton, 1936). See also Gerald L. Borchert, *John 1–11* in New American Commentary (Nashville: Broadman & Holman, 1996), 25–30 and "The Church's Proclamation" in *Tension: Empowering Christian Thought and Life* (Macon, GA: Nurturing Faith, 2021), 168–171; John B. Polhill, "Kerygma and Didache' in *Dictionary of the New Testament and Its Developments*, eds. Ralph P. Martin and P.H. Davids (Downers Grove, IL: InterVarsity, 1997), 626–29.

But as you probably know, the purpose statement (20:30-31) makes it clear that the stories in John are a "selection" and chosen for the purpose of challenging the reader (or storytelling listener) to believe in this Jesus, who is the Son of God, and that authentic believing should issue in a new way of life.

Before you encounter the stories themselves, please turn to my introduction and allow me to review some aspects concerning the nature of storytelling in general and perhaps some of my personal stories in particular. These might provide insight into my perspective on storytelling before I summarize for you the thorny issues of background, authorship, dating, and provenance for the Johannine gospel that I have detailed at length elsewhere.[4]

Then, as you begin the storybook itself, be ready for some fascinating twists and surprises that you may not have encountered in your previous studies or readings concerning this gospel.

Finally, friends, since the Church has historically symbolized the Gospel of John with an eagle, I trust that your thoughts will soar with the eagle as you read and reflect on these uniquely designed stories from the elder states-man of early Christians. May you be drawn to his lofty perspectives of what it means to know, confess, and live with the evangelist's captivating testimony that Jesus, the Christ, is indeed the dying-risen Son of God who takes away the sin of the world and offers to believers the gift of eternal life.

Welcome to this fascinating storybook. It is an inspiring book!

***

In concluding these preliminary remarks, you are no doubt aware that a preface is not merely intended as an appropriate place to indicate a writer's purpose or intention for a book. It is a convenient place to express the writer's gratitude to those who have been of assistance in bringing this work to fruition.

First, I want to express my continuing gratitude to God for the sustain-ing presence of Jesus through the Spirit in my life and for the encouraging companionship of my dear wife, Doris, in my writing. Both have been for me unmerited blessings for which I am truly thankful.

Then, I would mention that this work is gratefully dedicated to my former students and especially in this case to those at the Robert E. Webber Institute for Worship Studies. Students at the Webber Institute continually stimulated both Doris and me to become as creative as possible in directing them in their

---

4 See my extended discussion on these introductory matters in Borchert, *John 1–11*, 23–94.

learning processes so that all of us have been stimulated to use our God-given gifts to become the best ministers, worship leaders, and teachers under the divine tutelage of the Triune God. Thank you, dear students.

My sincere gratitude likewise extends to the Editorial Committee of the Webber Institute Books for their "enthusiastic" endorsement of this work. In addition, to those faculty members, alumni, and others who serve on this editorial board, including the general editor, Robert Myers, an esteemed former student, I remain deeply humbled that you again consider my work worthy of your high assessment. Thank you, committee members!

To those faculty members and administrators in various institutions both in the United States and Canada from various denominations who have read and commended my work at the front of this book, please accept my sincere gratitude for your very kind words. Your responses to my writing are most touching. Thank you, indeed!

Finally, I am grateful beyond words to both the editorial committee of Webber Institute Books for the unanimous approval of including my work in their Worship and Spirituality publications. I am once again very grateful to Bruce Gourley, the managing editor of Good Faith Media/Nurturing Faith, Inc. for negotiating the business aspects of publishing this manuscript. And I cannot thank Jackie Riley, my gracious editor, sufficiently for her great care and giftedness in bringing this third manuscript to press. She is a superb editor and is supported wonderfully by her associate, Cally Chisholm, in typesetting and artistry.

I offer a genuine "Thanks" to each of you for your kind spirit and dedicated work!

Introduction

The Majesty of Storytelling

A Puzzling Question and the Gospel of John

As I sat at my desk over the past months, I was repeatedly confronted with the haunting question: Why am I continually being called back to the Gospel of John? My basic assumption has always remained that Paul's works and the many other books of the New Testament have been exceedingly important to my life and teaching. Indeed, the other gospels are very significant in providing vivid insights into the self-giving life and the strategic death and resurrection of Jesus. But why am I being called back to John?

Reflecting on the Question

As I reviewed some of my earlier writings and particularly my work on the *Portraits of Jesus for an Age of Biblical Illiteracy*,[1] I thoughtfully responded to that puzzling question with the answer I have always been drawn to: Mark's picture[2] of Jesus as "mystery." His Jesus amazes all its readers, and his description of Jesus is nothing less than an awesome presence that shocked even his closest disciples with a fearful "God-likeness" (Mark 1:27, 2:12, 4:41, etc.).

In reflection, I added: I have continually marveled at Luke's beautiful portrayal of Jesus[3] as a caring shepherd who repeatedly rescues humans who are like wandering sheep that have strayed from the safety of the divine sheepfold (cf. Luke 7:9, 15; 8:48; 9:41; 10:41; 11:28; 15:3-7). Even on the cross, Luke's Jesus not only prayed for the forgiveness of his crucifiers but also granted a penitent criminal the hope of paradise. Then, I answered my question by asserting that I have always been enraptured by Matthew's representation of Jesus as the fulfilment of God's promises for all humanity (Matt 1:22; 2:3, 17; 3:3, 15; 4:14; 5:17; etc.). I added that the stuffy religious leaders of his day were merely hollow shadows alongside the authentic Jesus who embodied the meaning of *Torah* and what a true relationship with God entailed (Matt

---

1 See Gerald L. Borchert, *Portraits of Jesus for an Age of Biblical Illiteracy* (Macon, GA: Smyth & Helwys, 2016).

2 Please see the early work of David Rhoads and Donald Michie, *Mark as Story: An Introduction to the Narrative of a Gospel* (Philadelphia: Fortress, 1982).

3 See, e.g., the brief work of O.C. Edwards Jr., *Luke's Story of Jesus* (Philadelphia: Fortress, 1981).

5:17-20, 6:1-6, 8:18-22, 12:9-14, 15:1-9, 23:1-36).[4] But then I paused and again was confronted with: Why am I still being called back to John?

I know that each gospel has a unique portrait of Jesus and that each, under the guidance of God's Spirit, can assist in the transformation of our humanness into "God-likeness." Yet, I have kept wondering: Is there something in the strange complexity and simplicity of the Johannine stories that beckons me to return there? Then I asked myself: Does anyone else feel such a tug? Do you as a reader wonder about those stories? Well, I returned to John and reread those stories several times more. Then I remembered an incident from my past that had beckoned me to such a call.

A Clue from the Gospel of John

To help clarify what I have stated above, you need to know that I was born on Palm Sunday. So, as you might imagine, Palm Sunday has been quite special to me. Well, during one of my stints in Israel I was rereading the Johannine account and was in chapter 12 when I read the editor's subheading, "The Triumphal Entry into Jerusalem." Being present in Jerusalem at that time, I had witnessed the reenactment of the Palm Sunday parade, walked the earthy streets of the "Holy City," and watched a face-off between two priests of different Christian communities arguing about their time to control the tomb of Jesus in the Church of the Holy Sepulchre.

I stopped reading because I suddenly realized that the story in John had a strangely different focus than the other gospels. They had emphasized the "triumph." Yes, there is a hint of triumph in John among the crowd, but the focus is quite different in John. Instead, after listing the reactions of the crowd, the disciples, the religious leaders, and the Greeks, the Johannine story makes a sharp U-turn and indicates that the response of Jesus was: "The hour has come for the Son of Man to be glorified" (John 13: 23). Now, "glorified" might seem to imply "triumph," but John was purposely reminding his readers that such could happen only after Jesus had faced his self-giving "hour."[5]

---

4 See for example David E. Garland, *Reading Matthew: A Literary and Theological Commentary on the First Gospel* (New York: Crossroad, 1993) in which he introduces Jesus as "the Messiah, the Son of God."

5 Gerald L. Borchert, *John 12–21*, in vol. 25B, NAC (Nashville: Broadman & Holman, 2002), 39-56.

Reflections and Storytelling

With that memory in mind, I returned to my reading and reflecting. I began again to consider the nuances of storytelling, one of the supreme means that humans use to deliver or hand down to succeeding generations a sense of meaning or purpose for life. Stories may be true or fictional, imaginative or realistic. But one of the keys to effective and meaningful storytelling is whether the storyteller is able to entice the reader/listener into the thought world of the storyteller. The gifted storyteller must also be able to hold the reader's/listener's attention to the unfolding of the narrative. Several important questions follow:

- Is the plot sufficiently vibrant to claim the reader's/listener's continued attention?
- Can the reader/listener sense that the various segments or substories of the major story fit together as a unified narrative?
- Are all the characters merely "stick" or flat people, or is there a developing roundness to the presence of the major figures in the narrative?

What follows thereafter concerns the goals and relevance of the storytelling:

- Is the reader/listener able to determine in the overall narration either the stated or implied purpose of the storytelling?
- Can the readers/listeners identify themselves as being among those implied in the narrative, or are such implied connections fuzzy?

Failure on the part of readers/listeners to comprehend how they relate to the narrative and to its purpose means that the story/narrative may provide intriguing information to its "hearers" but may not accomplish the stated or implied purpose for the narrative.[6]

Before I venture further into discussing the Johannine storytelling patterns, however, let me illustrate some perspective on storytelling in general from my own life. Please consider these brief personal reflections, and then evaluate them in the light of some of the suggested criteria. There are several parts to

---

6 For an excellent discussion on narrative in the Fourth Gospel, see R. Alan Culpepper, *Anatomy of the Fourth Gospel: A Study in Literary Design* (Philadelphia: Fortress, 1983).

each reflection, so hopefully the process might give you some helpful insights into storytelling.

My Dad

When I was a boy back in Edmonton, Alberta, Canada, my younger brother, Don,[7] and I used to wait patiently (and sometimes not too patiently) for our dad to tell us another story about the indigenous people and the settlers on the Alberta plains during the early years before Alberta became a province. We would both climb up on our dad's knees as he sat in the big stuffed chair in our living room. When we both would have cuddled under his arms, we were ready to join him in the next episode of riding on a great stallion or investigating some strange tracks in the mud. Our imaginations went into high gear as our father's voice began his fascinating narratives. Dad was a great storyteller!

He was also a model Christian, who patterned his life on Jesus and who was almost as wise as the Apostle Paul. In fact, I do not remember a time when Dad failed to read his Bible at the beginning of the day. Indeed, when Don and I were both doing our doctoral work at Princeton, we would often remark to each other that we had just read something in one of the theologians that reminded us of Dad. Like all members of humanity, our dad was hardly perfect, but he was a terrific model and we learned firsthand a little of what Jesus must have been like.

Dad was patient, kind, and honorable, and seldom became angry unless someone was treated unfairly. He had hoped to go to seminary and become a pastor and share the stories of Jesus with others. Both Don and I knew that the stories he told us about Jesus were very different from his stories about the hardy new settlers on the plains and the brave, semi-nomadic people who inhabited the territory. The stories of Jesus did not grow out of his imagination: they grew out of the black-covered Bible he read every morning. I lost track of that Bible after Dad died, but as I was writing this new work, it strangely came in the mail without any address or comment. I do not know who sent it, but it has been very intriguing!

---

7 For those who may have encountered his later writings, my beloved brother is Donald M. Borchert, the editor-in-chief of the *Encyclopedia of Philosophy,* 2nd ed. (2006).

Dad did not go to seminary because money was scarce in his large farm family of a dozen children. Instead, he went to work at the big Swift plant in Edmonton. Soon thereafter he married our mother, who was an orphan and also the embodiment of trust and love. She filled Dad's heart with joy. Like many who came through the Depression of the 1930s, our parents resolved that their two sons would receive the best education they could afford so that hopefully my brother and I would serve God and humanity. Dad progressed rapidly in his work and after a few years was moved by his company nearly two hundred miles south to Calgary, where he became the manager of the Swift plant there. But Dad never forgot his longing to be a pastor and tell others the stories about Jesus.

Now that you have read a little story about my dad and my life, do you think my story had a purpose? Did it have an implied or suggested audience? If it had a purpose, what was it? And who do you think might be the implied reader(s)/listener(s) or suggested audience? These are the kind of questions that help us gain a little perspective on the magnificent storytelling author of the Fourth Gospel.

Otto A. Piper

The second storytelling reflection in my life involves Otto A Piper, a professor at Princeton who had an amazing story himself. He shared many details of his life with me when I became his graduate fellow and taught Greek to incoming seminary students. He also invited me to meet many of his well-known colleagues from around the world who came to visit him after World War II. Dr. Piper had been a revered multilingual professor of systematic theology and ethics at the University of Müenster when Adolph Hitler was coming to power in Germany.

Among the many stories Dr. Piper shared with me was the fact that when he was at the University of Göttingen around 1920, he read a commentary on Romans written by the Safenwill pastor, Karl Barth. Piper recognized immediately that the commentary was destined to become a classic, and although he was new at Göttingen, Piper became instrumental in bringing Barth to his school and the formal teaching profession. The two became close friends as they served there together for about five years. That friendship continued long after World War II when they visited with each other. Piper also shared a friendship with Albert Einstein, who likewise was brought to

Princeton after escaping Hitler's Germany. Since Piper and Einstein lived a short distance from each other, they would regularly walk to the nearby park and converse on one of the benches there.

When Dr. Piper moved to Müenster, his writings soon became known to the rising German inquisition. Nazi government agents subsequently visited him several times, particularly concerning his writings on Christian ethics. Finally, the day came in 1933 when the Gestapo informed him that he had twenty-four hours to get out of the country or he would be dealt with—probably sent to one of their concentration camps! He quickly packed and left for Great Britain, where he was welcomed and given visiting chairs of philosophy of religion in Swansea (1934–1936) and Bangor (1936–1937) Colleges at the University of Wales.

But that would not be Dr. Piper's permanent home. Dean Elmer Homrighausen of Princeton Seminary heard that Piper had been exiled from Germany, so he boarded a plane for Britain with an invitation for Piper to join the faculty as a visiting professor of New Testament in the fall of 1937. By 1941, Dr. Piper was installed as the Helen Manson Chair of New Testament Literature and Exegesis at Princeton, an honored post he held until he was named emeritus professor in 1962. In 1971 he was named Honorary President of the Society of Biblical Literature and Exegesis. He died in 1982.

Otto Piper influenced scores of doctoral students who became professors around the world, and his Friday afternoon teas for graduate students when he discussed many current, historical, and biblical topics with students and visitors became a legend at Princeton.

When I knew Dr. Piper, he had had two sons—and in that statement lies a remarkable story. When the Gestapo gave Dr. Piper one day to escape Germany, he was forced to leave one of his sons there. As a result, during World War II he had the strange reality of having one son in the German army and one son in the American military. As Dr. Piper continued telling me this story, he looked me squarely in the face and said, "Jerry, I know what God experiences when he has children on both sides of wars." Friends, I suggest you ponder that statement for a moment—a long moment! In that statement lies a hint at his understanding of what God has done in Christ. But then I was in for a shock: The name of the son who died in the German forces was named "Gero!" It was as though a lightning bolt hit me. I will never forget Dr. Piper's words and the look on his face.

Do you understand why that quiet-spoken, Christian gentleman has left an indelible mark on my life? He was a model of commitment to caring and integrity in the name of Christ. As a result of his faithful efforts in relief and the revitalization of Europe in the decade after the war, the Federal Republic of Germany honored him with one of its highest distinctions: the Order of Merit. During that time, he served as vice president of the American Relief Center for Europe and as president of the Emergency Committee for German Protestantism. Since those years at Princeton and because of Dr. Piper's influence, I have pondered much and written some about Christians and their relationship to the government. It is a subject that deeply concerns me in our fractured world of today.[8]

That beloved gentleman also greatly influenced my life in another significant way. Dr. Piper was committed to the spiritual strength that results from the unity of Christians. But he was fully aware that the leaders of the modern ecumenical movement had not paid sufficient attention to the "spiritual dynamic" that adheres to the quest for unity. So, he asked me and another former doctoral student to assist him with his book on *Protestantism in an Ecumenical Age*.[9] Working with Dr. Piper on that book stimulated many thoughts on church cooperation and ultimately led the leaders of the Baptist World Alliance to appoint me to the positions of secretary and then chair of their international Commission on Interchurch Relations.

Yes, I too believe that the church lacks unity! But I also believe that Christians generally lack the foundation for such unity, of which the Johannine storyteller reminds us clearly in 13:34-35—"love" is the key to unity. Love is one of the great themes of John's gospel. Indeed, loving one another is the called command or summons from Jesus that should be a characteristic of every Christian.[10] The "elder statesman" of the early church made that quality the defining characteristic of a Christian.[11]

---

8 For some of my recent thoughts on this subject, see Gerald L. Borchert, "Are Christians Captured by Culture or by Christ?" *Perspectives in Religious Studies* 48.3 (Fall 2021), 327–336; and "Living with Dual Citizenship," ch. 12 in *Tension: Empowering Christian Thought and Life* (Macon, GA: Nurturing Faith, 2021), 191–203.

9 See Otto A. Piper, *Protestantism in an Ecumenical Age: Its Root, Its Right, Its Task* (Philadelphia: Fortress, 1965), vi.

10 For my further discussion on the New Command of Jesus, see G. Borchert, *John 12–21*, *98–100*.

11 See my further discussions in "The New Covenant Characteristic: Tensions in Living the Way of Love," ch. 8 in G. Borchert, *Tension*, 113–125.

Now that you have read my second reflective story, what would you say concerning the purpose of this story and who might be the implied or suggested reader(s)/listener(s)? How would you characterize the persons named in the story: Are they flat or round? Did you learn enough in the short story to visualize the main character? What were his primary characteristics? Were they described in a compelling manner? What was missing in the description that would have given you a more captivating picture?

Israel

My third storytelling reflection is more involved and concerns not primarily a person, but a set of experiences that have impacted my life. As you read the story, consider these questions:

- Can you find one or more purpose(s)?
- Do all segments contribute to your understanding of its purpose(s)?
- Do any parts seem to be confused or fuzzy?
- What parts advance its purpose(s)?
- Are there any parts that do not advance its purpose(s)?
- Is there a main figure?
- To what extent does the main figure emerge as round or developed?
- Are there any stick figures?
- To what extent does the story emerge as a unified statement?
- Is there extraneous material that could be omitted without damaging the story?

Hopefully this exercise will help you to perceive just how skillful was the Johannine storyteller.

The incidents in this third story took place in my early professional life when I taught the Gospel of John as a visiting professor at the American Institute for Holy Land Studies in Jerusalem (now known as the Jerusalem University College). When I mentioned to Dr. G. Douglas Young, the founding president of the Institute, that I was interested in studying the relationship of the Gospel of John to the land of Israel, he immediately suggested that I should come as a visiting professor and teach a course on that subject.

I simply ate up my experiences there with the students as we visited many places and sites throughout the "Holy Land." When possible, I sought to give special focus to those sites that tradition suggests could be linked to Jesus and the Fourth Gospel. In those years, access to historic sites was not as restricted as today: For example, we spent several hours on the evening of Maundy Thursday in the *Cenaculum* (the late traditional site of the Last Supper) reliving those events in the story by flashlight. On another day, I took a group of students to view the Old City and its surroundings from the walls, looking down both inside and out, trying to reimagine places where Jesus and his disciples might possibly have visited.

Of course, it is important to remember that reimagining the Temple and the city in the time of Jesus and attempting to reconstruct the life of Jesus from the Gospels involves a great deal of speculation. Indeed, while the walls today may look very old, they are not the same walls as they were in the time of Jesus before the Romans destroyed much of the city in 70 (CE or AD) under Titus. Moreover, after the Bar Kochba(h) revolt was suppressed in 135, Hadrian had Jerusalem leveled and then reconstructed as a Roman city (*Aelia Capitolina*) in which the Jews were forbidden to enter.

[I must pause here briefly to add that because of new restrictions and political implications, it is unlikely today that professors would take students on some of our escapades, particularly around Jerusalem. There is a little more latitude for creative patterns of study in Galilee, but visiting large areas north of Jerusalem around Samaria and south around Hebron are generally restricted. Even Bethlehem requires special travel rules. On the other hand, I would add that since my time in Israel, places such as Caesarea Maritima, Beth Shean, and Tel Dan have been developed into wonderful sites for creative biblical and historical study, and climbing to the upper spring of Engedi (*Ein Gedi*) has not been restricted. So, it provides a rich opportunity for reflecting on the earlier stories of David and Saul.]

While in Israel, I had many other opportunities to learn about the people and the land, such as attending the celebration of the Samaritan Passover— which, in reflection, I would perhaps categorize as a fascinating combination of attending a rock festival and visiting a slaughterhouse. While I generally hesitate to condemn the worship of others, it was difficult for me in the contemporary world to comprehend how I might see the actions of the Samaritan priests as related to worship. I understand a little about ancient sacrifice, but their actions caused the words of Jesus in the story of the Samaritan woman to keep flashing in my mind: "You worship what you do not know" (John 4:22).

In contrast, my experience of flying at a low level over the land of Israel with Dr. Richard Cleave while he took hundreds of pictures for his photographic library was very enlightening. It provided some great insights into the land and helped me better understand Israel's history. I witnessed firsthand that places where the people of ancient Israel built their forts and fortresses to protect themselves from marauders and invaders was, in fact, often close to where the modern Israelis have built their checkpoints. These places were either a short distance apart or sometimes just across the road from each other, so that the ancient and modern strategies for defense were quite similar. Indeed, the modern Israelis often use the Bible as their source book for defense moves.

Like the Johannine writer, I could add many other stories concerning my teaching period in Israel and other later visits, such as attending briefings in the Knesset (the Israeli Parliament) with President Young of the Institute and other visiting professors from abroad. Especially instructive was observing how the members of the National Religious Party operate. But I will forego those other stories except for reflecting on my first visit to the Sinai.

When I was coming to the end of my teaching stint in Israel and spring was turning to summer, I had a special opportunity through the Albright Institute—where I had been studying about one day each week. Ora Lipschitz, one of Israel's foremost guides (who assisted the Israeli military in their conquest of the Sinai), agreed to lead a group of almost twenty English-speaking international professors on a camping trip through the Sinai Peninsula. My colleague, Carl Rasmussen, a former professor at Bethel Seminary, who was then a full-time teacher in the Institute and who had flown with me and Richard Cleave, also joined this unique camping adventure.

After boarding two six-wheel-drive command trucks, we headed with our baggage and supplies south past Jericho, Qumran, Masada, and Eilat into the desert where there were tracks in the sand but few roads. We slept in our bedrolls after scraping the ground each night to make sure we were not bitten by scorpions. And we reveled in the brightness of the starlit sky, even though we could hardly see our hands before our faces when the flashlights were turned off and the embers from our campfire had faded.

It was a marvelous trip that included many highlights such as climbing Jebel Musa (Mount Sinai) and swimming or snorkeling with colorful fish in the gulf and at Sharm-es-sheik (the southern tip of the Sinai). We were refreshed by the cool water of the great oasis and the shade from the giant palms at Wadi Feiran, and we were awed by Tuvia's Forest where volcanic ash had clustered around reeds that left straw-like holes through the hardened rock. We also endured the tedious climb on Serabit-el-Kadem, stopping for water several times at the instruction of our observant guide. When we finally reached the top, we found the ruins of the ancient temple dedicated to Hathor, the cow-goddess, who was the Egyptian guardian of turquois. Hidden between the mountain peaks was a well-preserved burial ground and Egypt's secret cave/mine that was a major source for the turquois used for making prized jewelry for the ancient Egyptian nobility.[12]

It was a camping trip like few others. And it reminded all of us of the Israelites' exodus from Egypt and their Sinai experiences. On the first night of our mobile trek, the well-known sociopolitical Old Testament professor Norman Gottwald suggested that each night we should retell some of the stories in the Bible as the ancient people of Israel probably did around their campfires when they traveled through the desert. The group immediately accepted his suggestion. Some of the discussions were rather thought-provoking, as differences of opinion were clearly voiced. Ora, our disciplined guide, quickly became our alarm clock not only for getting up in the morning and having a hardy breakfast but also for closing off our discussions and crawling into our sleeping bags at night.

Thus ends my third personal reflection, and it awaits your response. How would you evaluate it in terms of the questions I asked at the beginning of this reflection? But my mention of our evening discussions around the campfires naturally leads me to the subject of the Bible and oral culture.

---

12 For my more detailed discussion on the Sinai, see Gerald L. Borchert, *The Lands of the Bible: Israel, The Palestinian Territories, Sinai and Egypt, Jordan, Notes on Syria and Lebanon, etc.* (Cleveland, TN: Mossy Creek/Carson-Newman Press, 2011), 104–115.

The Stories of the Bible and Oral Culture

My experience in Israel, sitting around the campfire, has always caused me to remember how many stories in the Bible were formed in an oral culture and were probably told and retold from one generation to another before they were set down in writing. That fact, I would suggest, is why the stories of the Bible are so powerful. They have been filtered by repetition.

So, when I think of the stories in John's Gospel, I doubt they were first communicated in a written form. The Johannine author probably told those stories to many young and older believers alike, and the stories were probably seasoned over numerous years of retelling. They were hardly new literary creations such as those we might type on our computers, with the convenience of delete buttons for making revisions. By comparison, we live in a literary culture that writes out our ideas whether for publication in a book or dictating on the instruments of social media. Such a pattern of writing, however, was not the case in the time of our gospel writer. He grew up in a period when writing was expensive and usually served primarily as a recorded confirmation of business dealings or of previous reflections on important subjects.

When we consider the nature of such an oral culture, it is helpful to remember that Luke tells a story about the consultation or conference that took place in Jerusalem in which the legitimacy of Gentile believers was being hotly discussed (cf. Acts15). When the decision was finally made to accept those Gentiles into the fellowship of the early church without them first becoming Jews, the council recorded their decision into a brief letter, but they also sent Judas Barsabas and Silas along with Joseph/Barnabas and Saul/Paul to testify to the authenticity of their written record (15:22-29). For them, the spoken word from the mouth of living witnesses carried far more weight than the written record. But when the earliest witnesses were passing from the scene, those writings had to suffice. The Fourth Gospel was, I would argue, likely written during that transition period, and the colophon or testimony of authenticity that appears at the end of this gospel (21:24) must have served a similar confirming purpose.

To conclude this reference to orality, therefore, I would ask you to keep in mind how important the believers in the Johannine community regarded this gospel and its strategic stories. Remember that it was the community's leadership who purposely inserted the colophon at the end of the stories from the life, death, and resurrection of Jesus to affirm their authenticity. But the leadership also added an authentication that their beloved author/source/ witness had been at the cross and testified to the fact that "blood and water" had flowed from the pierced side of Jesus at the cross (19:34)! Two implications follow from that confirmation.

First, the resurrection of Jesus, for the believing church, could never be regarded as a fraudulent claim. Second, the death of Jesus was a reality, and it had a sacrificial significance for believers and for the church's proclamation. But I would also add that the meaning and significance of those words have been vigorously debated for centuries, to which I will return in my further analysis of this Jesus story.

In closing these personal reflections, I would again emphasize that, as we in the twenty-first century read these stories, we should remind ourselves that the ancient writer lived in an oral culture. He did not think as we do. To forget his setting will likely lead to our misunderstanding of those fascinating stories and their narrative contexts. Remember: our evangelist probably told those stories many times—before they were put into a continuous written form!

Introductory Issues and the Gospel of John

Before dealing with the majestic stories themselves, we must give some attention to the storyteller or the author and his narrative context. But to address the authorship, dating, and contextual issues means to enter a thorny briar patch that has consumed the attention of many authors. (In my larger commentary on John my discussion of these issues was trimmed to about seventy-five pages, but it could easily have been extended to twice or three times that length.)[13] Therefore, I will not here traverse that path. Instead, I will introduce the subject briefly and provide a summary of my perspective on those issues and then move on to discuss John's story of Jesus.

To begin, I should remind you that the term for "gospel" (the noun, *euangelion*) is derived from the Greek experience of messengers bringing, announcing, or proclaiming a message of "good news" (the verb, *euangelizethai*) to their recipients, and those messengers normally anticipated rewards for delivering their "good" messages. This term "gospel" is used by Paul frequently to designate his message ("my gospel"— namely, Rom 2:16) about new life in Jesus (cf. Rom 1:9, 16; 10:16; 11:28; 1 Cor 9:18; etc.). It is also used in both Mark (1:15, 8:35, etc.) and Matthew (4:23, 9:35, etc.) as a general meaning for the "good news" that has been given by God in Jesus. But the term does not appear in John—except in the title that was added later when the Gospels were being viewed more as a separate literary genre.[14]

As far as authorship of the Fourth Gospel is concerned, there are great differences of opinion on the topic. Leon Morris, who follows the traditional view, asserts that "throughout most of its history, the church accepted without question that the gospel was written by John the apostle."[15] Some more radical scholars, however, have not only rejected apostolic authorship but also dismissed the gospel outright as written by some unknown Christian in the second century, either because those analysts consider this gospel to be filled with myth and legend (cf. David Strauss and F.C. Baur) or because they view it as some type of hateful harangue against the Jews (cf. K. Kohler).[16] I would agree that this Johannine message focuses on the Jewish leadership, but the

---

13 See Gerald L. Borchert, *John 1–11*, in vol. 25 A, NAC (Nashville: Broadman & Holman, 1996), 23–97.

14 G. Borchert, *John 1–11*, 25–27.

15 See Leon Morris, "John, Gospel according to," *ISBE 2*, 1098–99.

16 G. Borchert, *John 1–11*, 81.

gospel is not a harangue against the Jews. Most scholars are far more nuanced in their acceptance or rejection of the Johannine authorship of the Fourth Gospel, for example, Raymond Brown and Rudolph Schnackenburg, both of whom had earlier supported the traditional view, but later changed their minds and have questioned the son of Zebedee's authorship.[17]

As for internal evidence, the gospel is vague as to who was the "beloved disciple." Tradition would favor apostolic authorship because of a few references such as those in Irenaeus—who believed the author was "John, the disciple of the Lord," the one "who leaned on his breast" (*Adv. Haer.* 3.1.2)— and in Eusebius—who reported that Irenaeus referred to Polycarp concerning his knowledge of "John" and "others who had seen the Lord" (H.E. 5.20.4-6).

But other aspects of external evidence are not as clear and, for some scholars, the general vagueness calls into question the apostolic authorship of the gospel. Alan Culpepper has provided a detailed account of this external evidence in his work, *John the Son of Zebedee: The Life of a Legend,* for those who would pursue this issue further.[18] But I would hastily conclude this section by stating that the suggestion of Pierson Parker concerning his idea that there was a confusion in the early church between John the early disciple and John Mark should be dismissed as speculation.[19] The alternative view of Floyd Filson[20] that the author was Lazarus is interesting, but is basically a creative construct. This proposal fails to recognize that Lazarus is a stick-like figure in the two closing stories of the first part of the gospel (see John 11:3, 33-36, 44; 12:9-11). My view is that this suggestion is an attempt to interweave the Lazarus stories with the stories of the beloved disciple, who in this gospel is used as a contrast to the rambunctious Peter—particularly in chapters 13, 20, and 21.

So, here are my beliefs regarding some of these introductory issues: (1) The prologue (1:1-18) and the epilogue (most of ch. 21) belong to the same author or authorial source as the rest of the gospel, but both segments were likely

---

17 Raymond E. Brown, *The Epistles of John* (Garden City, NJ: Doubleday,1982), 30–35 and *The Community of the Beloved Disciple* (New York: Paulist, 1979), 25–91. See also Rudolph Schnackenburg, *The Gospel of St. John,* 3 vols. (New York: Crossroad, 1987), who originally penned his first volume in 1965 (1.100–104) and changed his view in the 3rd German ed. (1975) to an anonymous figure (3.383–87).

18 See R. Alan Culpepper, *John the Son of Zebedee: The Life of a Legend* (Columbia: University of South Carolina Press, 1994).

19 See Pierson Parker, "John and John Mark," *JBL* 79 (1960), 97–110.

20 See Floyd Filson, "Who Was the Beloved Disciple?" *JBL* 48 (1949), 83–88 and *The Gospel According to John,* LBC (Richmond: John Knox,1963), 22–25.

written after the main body was completed. My thinking resonates to some extent with the words of Loisy—*"Le Livere est fini, tres bien fini!"*—but not with his implications.[21] On the other hand, I agree with B.F. Westcott's assessment (particularly his concern with the epilogue) that there is no substantial textual evidence to support a conclusion that these segments were missing in the transmission of this gospel. (2) The testimonials (19:35-37, 21:22-24) must have been added to the earliest manuscript before it was copied, as I have found no substantive textual evidence to the contrary.

I should also add that I believe the internal evidence (21:22-23) argues that the author or authorial source was an elderly man who was still living in the community, and perhaps the knowledgeable leadership there anticipated his imminent death. In any case, I am of the opinion that those early church leaders were certifying the truthfulness of their storytelling witness (19:35, 21:24). This conclusion leads me to the further assumption that John's gospel was likely written during the transition period between the early Christians' desire for oral testimonies from eyewitnesses concerning Jesus and the later period when there was a growing need for written testimonies about Jesus to be certified by the early church after most of the original witnesses were dying or had died. This time would coordinate with the time that scholars usually assign to the period following the insertion of the *Birkat ha Minim* (the early curse against Christians) that was added to the twelfth of the *Eighteen Benedictions* in synagogue services and with the third and fourth stages of Brown's concept of the Johannine Community and the presence of successionists, as I have argued concerning the Johannine epistles.[22]

Accordingly, I would put the date for writing this gospel in the time of Domitian or soon thereafter (the nineties of the first century or perhaps the beginning of the second century when persecution was a fresh reality). This period also coordinates well with the traditional view of authorship. But in arriving at this date, I would not thereby insist that the disciple John wrote or

---

21 A. Loisy, *Le quatrieme* evangile (Paris: Emile Nourrey, 1921), 514. I agree with Loisy that stories in the original organization of the book are finished at the end of ch. 20, but I believe the author soon realized that something needed to be added concerning Peter and the Beloved Disciple.

22 See Raymond Brown, *The Gospel According to John* (Garden City, NJ: Doubleday, 1966), lxxxiv–ix and *The Community of the Beloved Disciple* (New York: Paulist, 1979), 163–67. See also the discussion in J.L. Martyn, *History and Theology of the Fourth Gospel* (Nashville: Abingdon, 1979); M. de Jonge, *The Gospel of John in Christian History* (New York: Paulist, 1979), 90–121; and G. Borchert *John 1–11*, 45–49, 81–94.

dictated this document. Yet I think it is not far-fetched to believe that he was either the storytelling author himself or the authorial source for this gospel storybook. As a result, I will use the name John periodically in this work to mean either one of these options, and I leave it to you to choose which one you prefer as a result of your conclusions in further study.

I am also convinced that the author or authorial source was a Jew who was steeped in the Old Testament and the stories of Israel, that he understood the meaning of the Jewish festival calendar, and that he was among the people of Israel who were waiting for the coming of the expected Messiah. This reason, I believe, is why he was able to communicate so vividly how Jesus fulfilled the hopes of Israel in his stories. The Johannine storyteller was hardly a Hellenist whose background could be linked to Greek or Gnostic thought patterns as was suggested by Dodd, Bultmann, and others.[23] This writer was a committed son of Israel and hardly "a Jew-hater," as some others have suggested. He believed fervently that Jesus was God's promised answer to the plight of humanity and that the Jewish hierarchy had been self-centered and had betrayed their people—which is the reason his criticism of the Jewish leadership was so fierce.

[As a side note to the last paragraph, I would remind my readers that following the Second World War and the terrible Nazi pogrom of the Jews, some scholars thought that the Gospel of John needed to be cleansed of what they consider to be anti-Semitic (anti-Jewish) overtones. But I would remind myself and others that the Jews themselves killed their high priestly family during the destruction of Jerusalem by Titus. That family was not the epitome of authenticity. Stories of Annas picture him as a "godfather" whose lackies were not always people of integrity! I understand the attempt to cleanse the gospel of what may seem to be anti-Semitism associated with the scourge of Nazism. But I suggest that we remember the historical reality of Christians being hunted, as reflected in the curse of "the Nazoreans and *minim*" mentioned above. We cannot rewrite history! But we do not need to adopt hateful patterns that have followed poor interpretations of the text.][24]

---

23 See my extended discussion on "The Historical Milieu in Which the Gospel Was Written," in G. Borchert, *John 1–11*, 60–80. See Rudolph Bultmann, *The Gospel of John: A Commentary* (Philadelphia: Westminster, 1971) and C.H. Dodd, *The Interpretation of the Fourth Gospel* (Cambridge: University Press, 1958).

24 For the Jewish changes to their historical documents and their declaration of Christians as heretics, see C.K. Barrett, *The New Testament Background: Selected Documents* (London: S.P.C.K, 1956/Harper, 1961), 166–67.

The Johannine Storybook

With this brief review of the complex issues surrounding authorship, dating, and context in mind, I turn now to provide an overview or summary of how I see the stories in the Gospel of John have unfolded. While I continue to grow in my understanding of this Johannine testimony, I follow many of the summations and outlines of this text that I have developed in my earlier commentaries.

Overview: Part 1

The Johannine writer opens the first part of this fascinating story with John the Baptizer, the witness, who claims little for himself but who introduces Jesus, the central character of our story. Not only does the Baptizer introduce Jesus, but he also purposely turns over some of his own disciples to Jesus. And in sketching the Nathaniel encounter, he initiates the Jesus era (19:1-51) and prepares the reader for the beginning of the Cana Cycle and the first major division of our storybook.

This Cana Cycle then begins with two crucial episodes that provide important parameters for correctly interpreting our story. The first segment, a wedding event, identifies "signs" done by Jesus that serve as keys to recognizing who he is and the nature of his mission (2:11). The second episode, the cleansing of the Temple, provides parallel hints into that mission by revealing that Jesus' life will be consciously directed to his inevitable death and resurrection (2:22)—thus confirming the Baptizer's earlier proclamation of Jesus as "the Lamb of God who takes away the sin of the world" (1:29; cf. Rev 5:6-10)!

The remaining stories of this Cana Cycle then expand on the witness of the Baptizer who compared himself to a bridegroom and warned against identifying his role as that of the Christ or Messiah (3:27-30). Instead. as we continue, the Nicodemus story discloses that Jesus is the coming one who brings new life to mortals and is like God's serpent-sign in the wilderness that provided the way to healing for the early Israelites and for everyone who suffers from the serpent's wound of sin (3:14; cf. Num 21:9, Gen 3:1-7). Indeed, those who believe in Jesus can gain eternal life (3:36) because, as the Samaritans next testify, this Jesus is none other than the "Savior of the world' (4:42) and can remove humanity's thirst for the quenching water of life (4:15). Moreover, this Jesus, although unnoticed by most people, is present among hurting and dying humans when—like the father of the dying son—they cry out for healing (4:52-53).

The second cycle of our storybook encompasses the Johannine version of the Jewish Festival Cycle. It naturally begins with a focus on Sabbath since all the festivals are regarded as "Holy Convocations to the Lord" (cf. Leviticus 23). The first segment of this cycle revolves around a legal controversy over Sabbath that Jesus has with the Jewish religious authorities after he heals a complaining paralytic on the Sabbath. The face-off with those leaders then escalates during the Passover period to the issue of Jesus' identity. After Jesus surprisingly feeds the huge crowd of more than five thousand people with a boy's small lunch, the people are ready to make him king (6:15)! But when he announces that he is the bread of life from heaven (6:35) and that if they eat this bread (him), they will not die (6:50), his critics become so incensed that many followers withdraw their support. Indeed, Jesus even asks his disciples if they will also withdraw (6:60-67).

The popular festival of Tabernacles (7:2) is next crucial to our storyline. As a background, Jesus clearly refuses to accept his brothers' political challenge to declare his messiahship publicly at this festive season (7:3-6). And later when he faces the people and his critics continue to probe who he is, Jesus patiently refuses to violate God's determined "hour" (7:28-31). Yet Jesus does act: he simply makes a declaration.

Although it may not be obvious to contemporary readers, remember that Tabernacles came at the end of hot summers and special prayers for water had been added to the Tabernacle rituals because the cisterns of the city dwellers usually ran dry and needed divine intervention to sustain them in the time of drought. These prayers were dear to the Pharisees who even fought battles with the Sadducees over these rituals.

The Johannine storyteller obviously realizes the symbolic power of this side-story and therefore reminds his readers that on the "great day" of the feast Jesus proclaimed himself to be the source of "rivers of living water" (7:35-36). The opponents of Jesus would quickly realize the significance of this declaration (and many early Christians would have understood the meaning of the proclamation, too). Accordingly, it does not take long for a reaction to arise following the miraculous healing of the blind man to illustrating the antagonism.

But there is more to the increasing hostility! Tabernacles is also a time for celebrating freedom from Egyptian bondage, and for receiving God's law/

commands or Torah (8:12). So, when Jesus challenges the Jews to recommit themselves to freedom with his truth (8:31-32), that summons only creates a mushroom effect and produces an extended face-off related to truth, freedom, and being children of Abraham (8:33-59). Given this context, it is easy to understand why the storyteller uses the believing of the blind man as a powerful contrast to the unbelieving blindness of the Jewish authorities and as a means for introducing the strategic illustration both of the people's blindness and as an opportunity to deal with superficial perceptions about God and folktale answers to the questions of theodicy (9:2-3). Conflict is clearly mounting, and it is clearly evident.

With chapter 10 and the first *mashal* (extended parable) of the Good Shepherd during the winter festival of Dedication, the confrontations between Jesus and the religious leadership become intense because Jesus claims not only to "know the Father" (10:15) but also to be one with the Father (10:30). The Jewish authorities consider such a claim to be blasphemous, and they pick up stones to attack Jesus (10:31). Though Jesus leaves the scene unharmed, the confrontation with those leaders reaches the fever stage when Jesus demonstrates his divine power by bringing Lazarus back to life from the grave. At that point Caiaphas, the high priest, decides he cannott postpone acting and therefore makes the ultimate decision: Jesus must be sacrificed "for the people" before Passover (11:50-55). His decision brings the curtain down on Part 1 of our storybook.

Overview: Part 2

The Johannine storyteller sets the stage for our understanding of Part 2 as Mary opens our story by anointing Jesus with her valuable ointment. But the episode is made very ominous through two notes: the presence of the devilish Judas (12:4; cf. 6:70-71) and the fact that the anointing is for Jesus' "burial" (12:7). The storyteller then moves our attention to the entry into Jerusalem that suggests confusing reactions among the people until Jesus indicates that his death is as inevitable as seed dying so that fruit can be produced (12:24). These different reactions to Jesus introduce the reader to the third major cycle in our story.

The Farewell Cycle is truly a very creative piece of literature by the Johannine writer in which Jesus is first portrayed as demonstrating his servant nature when he washes the disciples' feet and gives them the command to love one another and to copy his life pattern (13:1-38). This cycle then ends with a majestic prayer in which Jesus enumerates his concerns and hopes for the disciples (17:1-26). Within these parameters Jesus is then pictured as acknowledging the reality of the disciples' loneliness and anxiety and as offering them not only divine solace and a future hope, but also the presence of the Holy Spirit who will support, comfort, teach, protect, enlighten, and guide them throughout their lives in the world (14:1-31, 15:28–16:33).

Then, in the second *mashal*—the centerpiece of this farewell message— the storyteller illustrates the relationship between Jesus and his followers. He is the vine, they are the branches, and the Father is the caring farmer. The focal point of this cycle then is highlighted by returning our attention to the great command of Jesus with its important implications (15:12-17). As you read these chapters, I am sure that you will agree that this Farewell Cycle is a literary masterpiece and provides a superb story link or transition from the confusing events surrounding the anointing and the entry into Jerusalem that followed the fatal decision of Caiaphas to the start of the Death Story that comes next.

The development of the Death Story contains another fascinating exhibit of the intriguing storytelling method. The author at 18:1-27 uses a series of brief modulating substories to move the main story forward rapidly. In using this method, the narrator repeatedly shifts the focus in this order:

From: Jesus' arrest in the garden
To: Peter's misconceived show of loyalty
Then to: the flawed trial of Jesus before Annas
Again to: Peter and his arrival at the charcoal fire with his first denial
Back again to: the trial of Jesus before Annas
Again, back to: the charcoal fire and Peter's final two denials

This substory concludes with the shrill crowing of the rooster (18:27). A somewhat similar pattern of modulation can be observed in 18:28–19:16, where the focus during Pilate's trial moves between the outside and inside of the praetorium (judgment hall) and the reader's attention is shifted between Pilate's argument with the Jewish authorities and his frustrated trial of Jesus:

Outside: The Jewish authorities deliver Jesus to Pilate.
Inside: Pilate confronts Jesus, and the trial quickly turns to issues of kingship and truth.

Outside: Pilate judges Jesus to be innocent, but when he tries to placate the Jews by offering to release either Jesus or Barabbas, they choose Barabbas.
Inside: Still trying to placate the Jews, Pilate has Jesus scourged.

Then the interaction continues, and the conflict becomes intense:

Outside: When Pilate displays the emaciated Jesus in a robe and a crown of thorns, the religious elite demand that Jesus be crucified.
Continuing Outside: Pilate tells the authorities to deal with Jesus themselves, which leads the Jewish leaders to change their charge from political treason to religious heresy.
Back Inside: Pilate is disturbed and questions Jesus, who does not answer. In his insecurity Pilate then threatens Jesus with his power, which leads Jesus to challenge Pilate's perception of power.
Continuing Inside: Jesus himself then renders a verdict that the process is twisted and the one who delivered him to Pilate is the guiltier person.
Outside: Pilate seeks to release Jesus, a move that is countered by the leaders who threaten to report Pilate to his supervisors and thereby eliminate his chances of gaining the coveted title of a "Friend of Caesar."
Continuing Outside: Pilate seeks to give his verdict in the case.
Continuing Outside: When Pilate asks the people for their opinion, they respond, "Crucify him!" When he asks again to be sure, "Shall I crucify your king?" they respond that they have "No King, but Caesar!"
Continuing Outside: The people's answer is clear, but it is their ultimate declaration of rejecting God (cf. 1 Sam. 4:4-8).
Continuing Outside: The case is closed. Jesus is condemned and delivered for crucifixion.

The account of the crucifixion of Jesus is quite brief. The charge (*titlon*) on the cross of Jesus is significant because the storyteller emphasizes that, despite opposition from the Jewish leadership, Pilate wrote "Jesus of Nazareth, the King of the Jews" in Hebrew, Latin, and Greek—languages that covered most of the classical world of that time.

The storyteller mentions two groups standing around the cross: the soldiers, who divide the personal garments of those bring crucified; and some from Jesus' band, including his mother and several other women and one disciple—the one on whom Jesus bestows the honor of caring for his mother.

Then, as Jesus is dying, he indicates he is thirsty and is given some sour wine (vinegar) to lick from a sponge. Finally, he utters the words that have reverberated through history: "It is finished" (John 19:30; cf. Rev 16:17, 21:6)—and he then "delivers" his spirit or dies.

But the storyteller is not finished with the Death Story. It is the day of "Preparation" before a high Passover that anticipates a cleansing of the land, so bodies should not be left unburied (Deut. 21:23). Accordingly, the Jewish leaders ask Pilate to perform the *crucifragium* (use the heavy mallet on the legs of the dying and thus dispatch those who might still be living). The soldiers follow their orders with the others who had been crucified with Jesus, but he is already dead. To make sure, however, one of the soldiers uses his spear and stabs the body of Jesus in the side, which results in blood and water flowing from the wound. The storyteller sees all these events as so significant that he pointedly authenticates these phenomena and views them as a fulfillment of Scripture. The burial is then completed by Joseph of Arimathea with the support of Nicodemus, who brings enough spices to bury a king!

We turn then to the resurrection stories. While the death of most heroes leads to the conclusion of most human stories, such is not the case with this story. Indeed, when Mary Magdalene arrives at the tomb early after the previous events, she discovers that the stone closure to the tomb's entrance has been removed. Hastily retreating from that scene, she finds Peter and the Beloved Disciple and informs them that the body has been removed and she has no idea where it/he is. The two disciples respond by running to the tomb, and after both view the grave clothes, the storyteller informs us that the Beloved Disciple believes. Mary later returns to the tomb, and this time she sees two angels who ask her why she is wailing. Her tearful response indicates her complete bewilderment at not understanding where the body is. But then someone beside her asks again: "Why are you wailing?" She tries to explain but is stopped cold when the person utters one word: "Mary!" Then she attempts to grab and hold on to him, but Jesus tells her that she should find the others and inform them that he is ascending to God. Mary obediently responds by carrying the good news of Jesus' resurrection to the others.

That evening the disciples assemble behind locked doors because of their fear. But locked doors are no problem: Jesus comes into their midst and greets them with the historic blessing of "peace." Then he commissions them to his mission of the forgiveness of sins and imparts the Holy Spirit to them. But Thomas misses that first Lord's Day blessing and, typical of a confirmed skeptic, insists to the others that for him to believe he needs genuine proof that Jesus is alive.

The next Lord's Day the situation is repeated, but this time Thomas is present. The risen Jesus singles out Thomas by calling special attention to the marks of his crucifixion. Thomas then declares the most significant confession in this Johannine storybook: "My Lord and my God!" But the storyteller wants his readers to understand that even if they did not see the risen Jesus, the Lord bestows a blessing on those who have "not seen and yet believe."

I believe that the first draft of this storybook then concluded with the brief defining purpose statement that reminds us that Jesus did many other signs that are not recorded here, but those included should lead us to believing who Jesus is and to gaining eternal life. That draft, however, was not the final stage of this storybook. Some other matters needed to be added—and they were!

The first additional segment is the epilogue, which contains a story reminiscent of the call of the disciples in Luke 5:1-11. In this Johannine addition, seven disciples return to their fishing but are unsuccessful in their all-night attempt to catch fish until a person on the shore tells them to cast their net on the right side of the boat. Then the net becomes loaded. When the Beloved Disciple identifies Jesus, Peter jumps into the water in his haste to reach Jesus. Later in a discussion around another charcoal fire, Jesus asks Peter three times if he loves hum. When Peter answers in the affirmative, he receives a threefold commission to care for the flock. But he also receives a foreshadowing of his coming martyrdom. Then drawing this epilogue to a close, the storyteller refutes the unfounded rumor that the Beloved Disciple will live until Jesus returns. This addition concludes with an authentication of this work and a summation of the anticipated significance of the storybook.

Then, I suspect that the final segment of writing this fascinating storybook is the prologue.[25] It is an incredible jewel of a mere eighteen verses that provides readers with one of the most elevated statements of Christology in the New Testament. Yet it does not diminish the role of God, who is here and in the main text of our storybook identified as the "Father." The primary focus of the prologue is to introduce the divine "Word/Person" who became flesh (human)

---

25 It reminds me of the way I wrote my doctoral dissertation at Princeton, and I have suggested this pattern to scores of my former doctoral students: When the draft of one's main work is completed, then it is much easier to finalize the introduction. Of course, most supervisors want to see if their students know where they are going before they begin to articulate the final format of the Introduction.

for a time and in his incarnate embodiment represented Godself to humanity as God's one and only Son. This Son came to enlighten humans, but he was tragically rejected. Yet for those who receive and believe in him, he authorizes them to become authentic children of God. Now while no human has ever seen God, this "Word/Person/Son of God" came to make him known.

What an intriguing story the Johannine storyteller has given to us! Are you ready to reflect with me more about its implications? After briefly scanning the outline of this fascinating story, let us consider further what the story-teller wants us to understand: Who is this Jesus, and why did he come to the world? But even more pointedly, I would ask you to consider what it means to "believe that Jesus is the Christ, the Son of God, and that believing, you may have life in his name" (20:31).

Part 1

The Bible's Transforming Storybook

Witness, Believing, and Conflict

Chapter 1

Introductory Stories of Witness
(1:19-51)

The Witness of the Baptizer
(1:19-28)

In its final form the Gospel of John opens with a magnificent prologue, which we will discuss at the conclusion of this fascinating book of stories. For the present, however, our attention is focused on the fact that the Johannine storyteller leads with his narrative about John the Baptizer, somewhat like Mark. While all four gospels have an early story about the Baptizer, the emphasis in the Synoptics is rather parallel whereas the emphasis in John's gospel is a little different.[26]

The story of John the Baptist in the Fourth Gospel begins with an immediate focus on an investigating committee sent from the Jewish religious hierarchy to ensure that John is operating within the appropriate boundaries of religious exercise. His response to their multiple questions is simple. He does not fit into their traditional categories, he is an outsider to their thinking, and he frustrates them. But his statement, "I am not the Christ" (1:20), is undoubtedly seen by the storyteller as a vivid contrast to the repeated refrain of "I am" that is a reference to Jesus throughout this gospel. The result is that while the other gospel storytellers use Isa. 40:3 primarily as a reference to the Baptizer being viewed as one who was preaching in the wilderness, the Johannine storyteller portrays him clearly in a conflict context in which an attempt is being made by the religious hierarchy to control his practice of baptism. Moreover, in response to the further question by the investigators of "Why are you baptizing?" (1:25), John informs those hostile religious authorities that they are in fact outsiders to the loop of divine knowledge (1:26). Yet in his humility (note the reference to his unworthiness in touching the sandals of the

---

26 See, e.g., Kurt Aland, ed., *Synopsis of the Four Gospels: Greek-English Edition of the Synopsis Quattuor Evangeliorum* (Stuttgart: United Bible Societies, 1979).

one coming), as an insider, he knows God's answer is strangely already in their midst.

Thus, in a very few words the Johannine storyteller has prepared the stage for introducing the triad of witnesses that follow.

Witnessing: A Triad of Stories
(1:29-51)

In these three brief stories (or pericopes) that are unique to John, the storyteller details an amazing number of names or characteristics for Jesus. As a result, the stories take on the role of a fascinating testimony concerning Jesus.

In the first story the Baptizer is identified as the gospel's prophetic witness who masterfully articulates the sacrificial purpose of God in sending Jesus as "the Lamb ... who takes away the sin of the world" (1:29). But even the Baptizer indicates that he did not know before the baptismal event that Jesus would be the expected messianic figure about whom he had been preaching. Yet, in the unfolding of God's will, when the Baptizer observes the descent of the Spirit upon Jesus (1:32-33), he becomes the strategic eyewitness to what could easily be described as the ordination of Jesus to his messianic role. The Baptizer not only proclaims the purpose of Jesus for humanity but also issues the stunning confession that Jesus is none other than the "the Son of God" (1:34). What a story to encapsulate the witness of John! But there is more.

The second pericope confirms the Baptizer's commitment to humility (see 1:27 for John's assertion of his unworthiness) as he selflessly recommends his own disciples to Jesus with a rearticulation of his earlier confession—that Jesus is God's Lamb and the sacrificial answer to the plight of humanity (1:36).

(If the subsequent conversation between the disciples and Jesus seems to be a little confusing in your English translation, I suggest that you treat the question of the disciples to Jesus "Where are you staying [operating]?" as their statement of interest in seeking to be his disciples and the response of Jesus "Come and see" as his acceptance of their interest [1:38-39].)

The implied result of the exchange is that former disciples of the Baptizer become disciples of Jesus.

One of those disciples, Andrew, immediately seeks out his brother, Simon, and gives him the enticing invitation "We have found the Messiah!" At that point the storyteller skillfully reminds his readers that the word "Messiah" has in fact the same meaning as their familiar name "Christ" (which the church added to the name of Jesus to designate his role as the "anointed" one of God [1:41]). When Andrew brings his brother to Jesus, the storyteller uses that special opportunity to remind his readers that Jesus is in the business of transforming humans and that Simon would become "Cephas" (which the church would quickly recognize as the name "Peter" [1:42]). Do you sense the skillfulness of the storyteller?

That skill is clearly displayed in the third story and the third "next day." The descendants of Israel were not unaware that God might deliver a message to them in three parts, and this pericope provides the capstone to the storyteller's initial accounts. (In interpreting these stories, please treat the three as an integrated unit and be careful not to focus on the three introductory phrases— "the next day." It is the storyteller's way of connecting the stories as a unit. If you fail to do so, you may encounter an interpretive problem when you come to John 2:1 and the "third day," which I will treat in the next chapter.)

After Jesus encounters Andrew and Simon, he decides to go to Galilee. There he finds Philip, who in turn finds Nathaniel. And like Andrew, Philip says they have "found" the one whom Moses predicted would be coming (1:45; cf. Deut 18:15). The foundational question is: "Who really finds whom?"[27] I think you will quickly agree that the disciples are hardly the finders! But I suspect that John is making a play on the word "find." Or do you think that humans might sometimes consider themselves to be in control—even of finding God?

But to proceed with our story, when Philip adds that Jesus of Nazareth is the long-expected prophet, that suggestion is too much for Nathaniel and he questions Philip's thinking process. Nazareth is hardly on Nathaniel's radar screen, but Philip does not argue: he simply echoes the earlier words of Jesus, "Come and see" (1:46; cf. 1:39).

The next part of this story provides one of the literary gems in the Johannine treasure chest. Jesus is clearly prepared for Nathaniel when he arrives. So, he announces to Nathaniel that although he gave the appearance of being a skeptic, he is an authentic (*alethos*, used adjectivally) Israelite devoid of deceit or guile (*dolos*)—unlike his duplicitous forefather Jacob prior to the Peniel experience with God (cf. Gen 32:24-30). That statement shocks Nathaniel, so he questions how Jesus knows him. The response of Jesus is classic.

---

27 See G. Borchert, *John 1–11*, 146.

Using the image of being under a fig or olive tree: Jesus indicates that Nathaniel is like a faithful rabbi who is committed to the study of Scripture or the Torah (1:48).[28] Nathaniel is both stunned and convinced that Jesus understands even his inner self. As a result, the skeptic becomes a believer and confesses with the Baptizer that Jesus is the "Son of God!" Indeed, he even confesses Jesus to be the "King of Israel" (1:49),[29] a theme that undergirds the entire Gospel of John and is highlighted in the crucifixion and burial stories (19:14-22, 39-40).[30] The impact of the storyline here is almost breathtaking in its scope, but the Johannine storyteller is not quite finished. He has more to add.

If Nathaniel thinks Jesus is an amazing analyst, he quickly learns that Jesus can stretch his mind much further. Indeed, the storyteller indicates that Nathaniel will witness a new sequence to the old Bethel story (in which the angels of God would now ascend and descend not on a place called Bethel ["house of God"], but on Jesus [cf. Gen 28:12]), because in his incarnation Jesus claimed the title of the New Adam, the true "Son of Man!" (1:51).

And with this conclusion to our reflection on this triad of stories that elsewhere I have called "Cameos of Witness,"[31] we turn to the "Cana Cycle" and the theme of "believing."

---

28 See Bultmann, *The Gospel of John*, 104.

29 For my further discussion, see G. Borchert, *John 1–11*, 147–149.

30 See my discussions of the idea of Jesus being the king in the crucifixion and burial stories in G. Borchert, *John 12–21*, 255–61, 264–66, 281. Cf. the burial of Rabbi Gamaliel in Str-B 2.584.

31 See G. Borchert, *John 1–11*, 133 and "John" (1995), 1048.

Chapter 2

Stories of Believing and the Cana Cycle
(2:1–4:54)

A Surprising Wedding with Jesus
(2:1-12)

Now we come to our interpretive surprise: "the third day." Why not the fourth day? We have had three "next day[s]" already. But remember, the triad is a unit and we are moving to a new emphasis. The answer lies in an ancient Jewish tradition concerning marriage, which takes us back to the opening chapters of Genesis and the stories of creation. You may recall that it was on "the third day" the ancient Genesis storyteller indicated God saw that "it was good" twice on that day. As a result, many later Jewish couples considered that the third day would bring an extra blessing if they were married on this day!

The wedding at Cana begins the first of our three major cycles in Cana. (This cycle will also end in Cana, creating what literary critics designate as a storyteller's *inclusio*, or an inclusive segment.) The wedding is full of surprises, for example:

1. The preparations are inadequate.
2. The mother of Jesus, who remains unnamed, is apparently in charge of the preparations.
3. In frustration the Jewish mother calls on her son to help solve a problem.
4. This Jewish son who loves his mother and will care for her—even when he would later agonize in death (cf. 19:26)—reminds her that his life is not directed by earthly relationships but by a divine relationship and an appointed "hour" (2:4).
5. The mother understands her son's gentle critique and informs the servants to follow his directions (2:5).
6. Jesus instructs the servants to fill six huge, stone, purification jars with water and take some to the director of the feast (2:8).

(How much water is turned into wine and used at the feast is a matter of speculation, but probably between 16 and 27 gallons.[32] From the director's perspective, it is blue-ribbon wine in quality and not the kind of wine that would usually be offered to guests after they have already imbibed a good deal of cheaper wine and would not recognize the difference [2:10].)

[I must pause and add a note concerning an experience of one of my sons who came home one day and told me that his teacher had studied Greek and that the Greek word for "wine" (*oinos*) meant non-alcoholic wine. I had some idea what the teacher was trying to do, but I looked at my son and said: "Son, I teach Greek!" That Greek word clearly means an "intoxicating beverage," and the context implies they had been drinking wine (cf. 2:10). Then I continued: "You know, I do not drink alcohol, but your teacher does not know what he is saying on this matter. He is a fine young man who is trying to serve God, but I want you to be discerning about truth and where you get your information. You see, many people want to twist the Bible to fit their presuppositions. You are in high school now, and I am going to see if we can get you into a Greek class here at seminary with one of our younger teachers. Friends, my response to the teacher's statement is: let's be honest about what the Bible does and does not say!]

So, what do you conclude from this story? In case you are wondering, John hints at what the story means. It is the key (*archēn*) to understanding the signs (*semeia*) in his gospel. Somehow, in this event, Jesus "revealed" something of his "glory" (*doxa*) and the "disciples believed in him" (2:11). Have you ever wondered what that statement means? That experience must have been something of an epiphany for the disciples. They must have sensed something unusual about Jesus, something they could not quite figure out, something we might say was a little spooky—which is partly what "glory" also means. We often think that glory means bright lights and halos, but the Hebrew *kabōd* carries with it a sense of power and heaviness that cannot be explained naturally. I suspect that is what the evangelist was trying to say in this story. This section of John is about believing, but what did the disciples believe at this point? The answer here may have been a bit dubious for them, but I think you will find their "believing" will unfold as we continue the story.

In the meantime, the evangelist transitions the mother of Jesus, "his brothers," and the disciples very briefly from the hill country of Cana down some

---

32 See G Borchert, *John 1–11*, 156.

600 feet below sea level to Capernaum and the Sea of Galilee (2:12) before Jesus and the disciples move next to Jerusalem (2:13). But in doing so he has raised a hornet's nest that I will pause briefly to address here.

The mention of the brothers of Jesus flies in face of the theology of the perpetual virginity of Mary that is espoused by many Christians in both the East and the West (Roman Catholics, Orthodox, and some Anglicans). Raymond Brown represents the view that the brothers of Jesus are the sons of Joseph prior to his marriage to Mary, a view that goes back to Epiphanius.[33] A less-followed alternative is that these "brothers" were cousins of Jesus and the sons of Joseph's brother (or perhaps his sister), a view that was advocated by Jerome.[34] The general Protestant interpretation is that "brothers" implies they were later children of Joseph and Mary and were, therefore, half-siblings of Jesus.[35] I have commented on this issue elsewhere and therefore will pass on it here because it does not relate directly to this storytelling work.[36]

Shifting the Cleansing of the Temple and Its Implications (2:13-25)

The next story, the cleansing of the Temple, seems to be out of place in John because in the other gospels it is treated during the last days of Jesus' ministry. The result is that some interpreters, who are bound by chronology, think there must have been two cleansings. But there is only one cleansing in each gospel. What then is happening in John?

The answer is that John is a magnificent storyteller! Like some of our contemporary television programmers, John takes the strategic episode in the life of Jesus that sets the stage for his death and uses it early in his story to signal that a major problem is ahead in the full story. Indeed, John has placed it almost at the very beginning of this gospel: he knows the purpose for the coming of Jesus, and there is no changing that purpose. (In the study of drama, we have historically called such a planned shift of a segment in a narrative as

---

33 See Raymond E. Brown, *The Gospel According to John*, AB (Garden City, NJ: Doubleday, 1966, 1970), 1.112.

34 See G. Borchert, *John 1–11*, 159 for several views.

35 See, e.g., Leon Morris, *The Gospel According to John*, NICNT (Grand Rapids: Eerdmans, 1995),187–90.

36 For my views on sinlessness, see G. Borchert, "The Virginal Conception and the Incarnation" in *Jesus of Nazareth: Background, Witnesses, and Significance* (Macon, GA: Mercer University Press, 2011), 217–20.

"In medius res" ["in the middle of things"], and in modern television we usually refer to it as "flashback.")

Thus, the Johannine evangelist has taken the Passover, the crucial marking point in the mission of Jesus, and placed it at the start of this pericope! So, do not think for a moment that John was confused chronologically. He knew what he was doing, and we must try to follow his thinking. When he wrote his gospel testimony, it was many years after the event. John already knew that Jesus had died and was raised from the dead. This story, therefore, is used as a prefiguring of what is to come—which is exactly what he says in 2:22 when he wrote "When he was raised ... the disciples remembered." This verse supplies a post-resurrection perspective for believing in the ministry of Jesus, just as the entire gospel does.

What then is the point of moving this story forward? It is to let the implied reader know that Jesus understood from the beginning that he was fulfilling and replacing the Jewish pattern of worship. How do we know that fact? Jesus rejected the Jewish use of the Temple as an unholy marketplace (a corrupt business that developed from the exchange of money for purchasing animals with temple currency based on an interpretation of Deut 14:25-26). The practice supported not only worship costs, but also other activities. In disgust, Jesus turned over their "tables" (John 2:15; *trapezas* is the.Greek word for banks even today). But the evangelist goes much further in making this point by using a Greek play on the words for "Temple." He refers to the Temple generally as *hieron* (2:14), but when it means the inner sanctuary—the *naos* (2:19)—he does not mean the Most Holy Place. Instead, the sanctuary of worship is now to be understood as the person of Jesus. The message in the story is unmistakable: Jesus is the new center of worship!

But if you think that idea is too radical, read the three-verse conclusion to this pericope. In it John first simply states that many people believed when they saw the signs Jesus did (2:23). But then comes the shocker. (To explain what I mean, let me say that I have read countless commentaries that try to explain the next statement. Frankly, I think many of them skirt the issue—whether it is in their attempts to distinguish the tenses of the same Greek verb *pisteuein* ["believe"] or some other thesis.) I think John is saying that "Jesus did not believe in their believing!" Really? Did John say something so radical? Yes, I think he did: John tells his readers in the next verse that Jesus knows humans to their core, and he knows when believing is authentic and when it is not (2:25). Humans do not fool Jesus, a fact that sets the stage for the next pericope: the Nicodemus story.

Nicodemus and the Night Encounter
(3:1-21)

Our story opens with what seems to be a rather formal introduction of an important official by the name of Nicodemus, who by all indications is a leader among the Jews (3:1). But the tone quickly changes with the arrival of darkness and Nicodemus is presented as coming to Jesus "by night" (3:2). (Note that time and weather designations in John are more than peripheral realities: they usually carry spiritual overtones.)

Although Nicodemus may be a religious leader, the Johannine evangelist wants us to understand that "Nick," as we could call him, is in fact in the darkness. Yet the formalities continue, and Nicodemus attempts to use convenient "God talk" with Jesus because he knows that no one can do the "signs" Jesus does "unless God is with him" (3:2). (Note that the word is plural, but Jesus has only done one powerful sign according to John. So be careful how you deal with numbers and chronology in John. Do not take your order from the Synoptic Gospels or from your current Western understanding of chronology.)

Jesus is not misled by fancy God-talk, so he turns the conversation on its head by announcing to Nick that "unless one is born anew/from above (*anōthen*), he cannot see the kingdom of God" (3:3).[37] That response completely shatters the formalism of Nicodemus, and in bewilderment he questions such a possibility of a new birth for an elder statesman. His only response is a retreat to his understanding of the natural birth processes.

But Jesus is not tied to phenomenological thinking. Instead, he points this religious leader to the existence of authentic spiritual realities such as

---

37 The expression "Kingdom of God (or Heaven)," which is used frequently in the Synoptic Gospels, appears only here in John 3:3 and 3:5. The preferred Johannine expression seems to be "eternal life."

water and the Spirit that do not quite fit rationalistic thinking (3:5).[38] Thus, Jesus is attempting to point him beyond his current mindset. Accordingly, the storyteller challenges his readers to reflect on the meaning of eternal life and salvation, which here is described as being "born from above/anew"—an idea that Jesus seems to imply as related to being "born of water and the Spirit."[39]

When Nicodemus cannot comprehend those spiritual realities, Jesus returns to the phenomenal world of "wind" to remind the religious leader that the wind is like the reality of the Spirit.

But when Nicodemus has difficulty fathoming the discussion, Jesus is forced to conclude that, as a teacher of Israel, Nicodemus hardly understands and believes earthly realities. How then is it possible for him to believe in heavenly realities such as the Son of Man's descent from heaven (3:8-13)? Indeed, the question set before Nicodemus and all humanity concerns whether we, in fact, understand the saving power of God. Thus, just as Moses, under the instruction of God, raised (lifted up) a bronze snake in the wilderness so that those who believed in God's power would be healed of their earlier snake bites and live (cf. Num 21:8-9), so also Jesus says that he will have to be lifted up (be crucified) in order that those who believe in him may gain eternal life

---

38 I would note here that that the expression "water and the spirit" has been the subject of considerable controversy. Scholars such as Rudolph Bultmann (*The Gospel of John*, 139) and Ernst Haenchen (John, 1. 218, 227) have argued that the addition of "water and" is the work of an ecclesiastical redactor, but such a suggestion is a subjective conjecture that focuses not on the text but assumes to rewrite the story for the evangelist. Others argue that water here refers to baptism, and they attempt to support their idea by a reference to 3:23, but that suggestion imports the idea from the next pericope that deals with the subject of a comparison between Jesus and the Baptizer—which again is a questionable methodology.

39 So, the big question is: Does "born of water and the Spirit" refer to Christian baptism? As I have argued in an excursus on "Baptism," the answer is rather nuanced. Birth from above and born again definitely are related to eternal life in John. And in the early church, "baptismal" imagery is frequently used to reflect the salvation process as Paul suggests of being "buried and raised" with Christ in Romans (6:1-11). The expression of "putting off" old ways and "putting on" Christ and new life certainly is a pictorial representation of the baptismal experience of new converts as they would put on new clothes (see, e.g., Eph 4:22-25 and Col 3:5-17). But what is crucial in our thinking is to realize that both baptism and salvation are not simply either a divine or a human action, but a combination to bring about a transformation of humans in our world and society through (1) divine action and (2) human will within the (3) context of a Christian community. Focusing on only one or two elements of this triad will ultimately lead to the skewing in our understanding of Christian baptism. For my further discussion on baptism, see G. Borchert *John 1–11*, 174–76.

(John 3:14-15).[40] Of course, we know that the bronze serpent did not heal the people of Israel. It was God, so we must expand our dimensions of thinking.

The mention of "eternal life" then serves the storytelling evangelist the basis or key word for introducing the best-known verse in the Bible concerning God's love and God's gift of eternal life through Jesus (3:16). But more importantly that reference to eternal life also provides the basis for introducing the entire crucial six verses concerning a balanced perspective between love and judgment that brings the Nicodemus story to a conclusion (3:16-22). It is not an adequate representation of the gospel merely to quote John 3:16, because the next verses are critical to the witness of this gospel.[41]

The gospel story is clearly about God's love for humanity, but it is also about the tragic human rejection of that love and the consequent judgment or condemnation that has followed. Yes, God loves the world and gives eternal life to those who believe in Jesus (3:16-17). No, most of the world does not respond to God's love and therefore humans are condemned—already (3:18). Yes, God gives love and enlightenment to humanity. No, humans do not accept God's love: they prefer their evil practices to the love and enlightenment of God (3:19-21).

But the story of Nicodemus is here left hanging for the present. Did he join the Jesus group, or did he remain in darkness? For the answer to those questions, we must wait for further enlightenment. In the meantime, however, we must return to John, the Baptizer, and his witness, to check on his continuing role in this ongoing saga.

Questioning Parallel Ministries: The Baptizer and Jesus
(3:22–4:3)

John the Baptizer was apparently still around when Jesus began his ministry. Indeed, some scholars have suggested that John was in prison before the Galilean ministry of Jesus took place.[42] But according to the Johannine

---

40 Here is the first use of "eternal life" (*zoē aiōnios*), which is used seventeen times in John. It is used only once in the Greek of the Old Testament (LXX) at Dan 12:2 (12:7).

41 See G. Borchert, *John 1–11*, 183–86.

42 Rudolph Bultmann (*Gospel of John*, vii–xii), in the light of his view of this gospel, pursues a series of textual displacements and glosses or creations by the evangelist. For an analysis of this issue, see Walter Wink, *John the Baptist in the Gospel Tradition* (London: Cambridge University Press, 1968), esp. 93–99.

evangelist, the Baptizer had "not yet" been imprisoned (3:24) and not been beheaded by Herod Antipas as the result of the treacherous schemes of Herod's second wife, Herodias (cf. Matt 14:1-12).[43] Furthermore, whatever may be your view of displacements in this gospel, the question soon arose: Were the ministries of John and Jesus to be viewed as parallel? It was a question among John's followers that would continue after the death of the Baptizer. Bultmann and others, accordingly, have linked the Baptizer's disciples with some later baptizing groups, such as the Mandeans.[44] But such a direct linkage is speculative.

The question of parallel ministries, however, was an issue that the Johannine evangelist obviously felt needed to be settled because the early Christians were encountering disciples of John who continued to preach the baptism of repentance, as John had earlier instructed (cf., e.g., Acts 19:1-6). Therefore, to treat the issue directly and preempt any arguments that Jesus was merely a follower of the Baptizer, the evangelist includes what he considered to be a brief conclusive reflection from the Baptizer's personal testimony to his disciples. Using his own phrasing in an emphatic form, the evangelist asserts that "I am not the Christ" (*ouk eimi egō ho christos*) "but I have been sent prior to that one" (3:28; cf. 1:20, 30).

To make this testimony more emphatic, the evangelist uses a typical Jewish parable of a bridegroom and the friend of the groom who waits outside the bridal chamber for the voice of the groom to confirm the fulfillment of the marriage and then announces its consummation to the expectant wedding guests (3:29). And if that testimony of the Baptizer was not sufficient, the evangelist adds: John witnessed that Jesus had to increase but that he had to decrease (3:30). And to cap the testimony, the Baptizer asserted that Jesus is from above/heaven and is above all, whereas he, the witness, belongs to the earth and the terrestrial realm (3:31).

Therefore, the ministries of Jesus and John were not parallel. The storyteller tried his best to convince everyone that their ministries were on totally different planes—just as the Baptizer had done earlier (1:26). But he concludes that people believe what they want to believe and even the "signate seal" of God's "truth" (*alethēs*) may not change their believing (3:33).

---

43 For insights into Herod Antipas and the intrigues of his second wife Herodias, see Harold Hoehner, *Herod Antipas* (Cambridge: University Press, 1972).

44 Bultmann, *Gospel of John*, 88, 170–71. See my further comments on Gnosticism and particularly on the Mandeans in G. Borchert, *John 1–11*, 76–80.

It is difficult for this evangelist to understand why people, especially his own people, rejected Jesus (as he indicated in the summarizing prologue, 1:11), even as Paul had difficulty understanding the failure of the Jews to accept Jesus (cf. Rom 9:1-6). But both witnesses had to learn to accept the painful reality of this rejection of Jesus, and they had to expand their vision for the proclamation of the Good News to the world (Rom 10:8-10, John 1:12). The result, as the evangelist here declares, is that those who believe God's Son receive eternal life. But those who do not obey God's Son will not experience life. Instead, divine indignation or wrath will continue to settle on them (3:36). These reality statements thus provide a window into the conflict that Jesus will face in the upcoming Festival Cycle and the rest of the gospel.

But another hint of the upcoming conflict is suggested with the transition verses that begin chapter 4 when the evangelist informs us that the popularity of Jesus is growing in comparison to the Baptizer and the Pharisees are taking notice. So, Jesus and his disciples leave Judea and head north (4:1-3).

Do you sense how important believing in Jesus is for the storyteller? What about for the Samaritan rejects and others? These questions lead us to our next stories.

Confronting a Samaritan Woman and Its Significance (4:4-42)

As with many of the priceless Johannine stories, once you read them, they remain simmering in your mind awaiting your periodic decisions concerning their current implications for life. Such is the case with our next story. It can lead your reflections in many directions, such as: your relationships with others, your decisions about what is primary in life, the ways you seek to avoid confronting reality, and even what you will call Jesus.

Like most good storytellers, the evangelist provides links between his stories. In this case, it involves a transition that carries his readers from the fact that the Jesus group is already making more disciples than the Baptizer's group—although the evangelist wants everyone to know that Jesus is not primarily in the baptizing business (4:2). (Much like Paul, who followed the lead of his Lord, Jesus did not discount or diminish the importance of worship practices such as baptism, but he also did not focus on that ceremony; cf. 1 Cor 1:16.) Then, the evangelist adds, for some undisclosed reason (divine or otherwise), that it is necessary (*edei*) for Jesus to "go through"[45] Samaria to get to Galilee (John 4:3-4)[46]—which brings us to the context of our next story.

In the Old Testament, local wells were typical places for important meetings. The mention of Jacob's well by the storyteller in John is a natural connector because Jacob was the patriarch of both the Samaritans and the Jews (4:4-6), and the well is a perfect place for a meeting. The time of day, although approximate,[47] is also important. At the sixth hour, near noon and in the heat of the day, Jesus sits down beside the well. He is tired (4:6)!

The storyteller begins the narrative by simply saying that a woman of Samaria comes to the well to draw water. But before the woman makes her appearance, the evangelist notes that the disciples have conveniently left the scene to buy some food for the weary travelers. Meanwhile, the unsuspecting reader, like the woman, is in for a surprise. Women did not normally come to the well to get their supply of water in the heat of the day. But do you think this woman expected to meet a man there, particularly a Jewish man—who would ask her for a drink (4:7)? His request starts a fascinating conversation. As we soon learn, she apparently does not have difficulty talking to men because she probes the reason why Jesus, a Jew, would readily talk to a Samaritan woman—who would probably be at the bottom of the list of appropriate people with whom a Jewish man would converse (4:9). Samaritans were regarded negatively as half-breeds by Jews.[48]

It is, however, the perfect opening for Jesus, and he offers her "living water" (4:10). Now the woman is intrigued by this man. She probably thinks his response may be a new approach, so she probes him further about his missing bucket and his source of living water. Then she must be thinking out loud, "Could this fellow be greater than our patriarch, Jacob, who supplied water for his entire family and animals?" (4:11-12).

Now Jesus has her attention, and he informs her that his living water is very different from the well water that needs to be replaced daily. His water is like a bubbling spring providing "eternal life" (4:13-14). She responds with

---

45 The verb *dierchesthai* seems to emphasize the fact that most Jews passed through but did not stop long in Samaria.

46 For my further discussion of the frequently suggested idea that most Jews took the long route around Samaria to get to Galilee, see G. Borchert, *John 1–11*, 199.

47 For my further discussions on time, see G. Borchert, *Tension*, 7–9, 142–54.

48 For the account of Josephus concerning Samaritans, see his Antiquities, 9.277–91. See also J. MacDonald, *The Theology of the Samaritans* (London: SCM, 1964) and R.J. Coggins, *Samaritans and Jews* (Atlanta: John Knox, 1975).

something akin to: "Give me this water, so that I will no longer be thirsty—and have to pull up this old well-water" (4:15). She hardly knows at this point where this conversation is headed, but Jesus is ready to inform her!

Jesus directs her to "Go, call your husband, and come here" (4:16). Perhaps thinking, *what is going on with this guy?* she snaps back, "I have no husband!" Jesus is hardly shaken by her harsh reply and simply says: "You are correct … You have had five husbands, and the one you are living with now is hardly a husband" (4:17-18). Likely gasping at the detailed accuracy of his account, she quickly recovers, however, and tries to change the subject and focus on a common argument (which still is used today): "Where is the best place to worship? We Samaritans say it is here on Mt. Gerizim, but you Jews think it's in Jerusalem." Jesus responds in laser-like fashion: "The determined time is approaching when neither place will be primary in worshipping God." In the interim, he could tell her: Samaritan worship is quite confused, whereas Jewish worship is historically closer to God's intended desires for humans. Nevertheless, he continues: "The time is fast approaching and, in fact, is here" when authentic worship of the Father will be "in spirit and truth." That is the kind of worship God expects from humans (4:21-24).

Not taken back by the eschatological (futuristic) thrust of his response, the woman must be thinking: I can counter his attempt to teach me by asking him the real eschatological question. So, she tries to upstage Jesus by indicating that she knows something about the future, namely that "the expected one" is coming, the one whom the Jews call the "Messiah/Christ" and the Samaritans call their *Taheb*.[49] Moreover, she says, "when he appears," he will reveal everything! Her response does not shake Jesus: He simply answers with the repeated story theme, "I am" (*egō eimi*,). "You are speaking to him" (4:26)!

With these climactic words, this intense conversation ends. And like a great storyteller, the evangelist switches the scene to the return of the disciples. They are stunned that Jesus is talking to a Samaritan woman, but they remain temporarily silent, while their questions are left unspoken. Not so with the Samaritan woman: she quickly leaves the scene and her water pot (4:28) and goes off to inform the men (*anthrōpois*) of the city! "Come see a man (*anthōpos*), who told me all the things (*panta*) I have ever done." Then she adds, "Could this one be the Messiah?" (4:29). (Ponder for a moment: Do you

---

49 See G. Borchert, *John 1–11*, 209. See also John Wick Bowman, "Samaritan Studies" in *Bulletin of the John Rylands Library* 40 (1957–58), 298–329, esp. 298–300.

think the men *and* the women of the city might be interested in meeting this Jesus who had captured the attention of this loose woman?)

Back at the well, the disciples are concerned about their purchases and want Jesus to join them in eating. Instead, Jesus tells them, "I have food of which you are not aware" (4:31-32). His words puzzle them. Their minds are stuck in the phenomenal world, so they try to discover if someone has brought him food. In response, Jesus states that his food is to do the will of the one who sent him and to "complete his work" (4:33-34). Then, using agricultural images as he does in many discussions, this conversation with the disciples is strung together with several maxim-like statements concerning sowing and reaping and the joyous sense that comes to the laborers who respond to his summons for working together in the harvest fields (4:35-38).

The story then masterfully concludes in four brief verses by reintroducing the Samaritans who first "believed" because of the woman's testimony: After inviting the travelers to "remain" with them for a short time, they "heard" from Jesus themselves and came to "know" him. Then these so-called Samaritan rejects issue one of the primary confessions in the gospel, namely, that Jesus is "truly the Savior of the world" (4:42).

The Unusual Healing of an Official's Son
(4:43-54)

The final story in the Cana Cycle brings us back to Galilee after a short visit in Samaria (4:43). The stories are here connected by a three-verse saddle that links Samaria to Galilee. But the middle verse of the saddle contains a strange, almost parenthetical, maxim-like statement concerning a prophet not receiving honor in his "home area" (*patris*). Some commentators treat linking texts like this one as seams in ancient narratives and often view them as the work of pedantic editors or redactors who lack creative literary gifts, but I am not fully convinced by these evaluations concerning the Johannine evangelist because most of the other linking texts are extremely significant. Yet this seam and the conclusion to chapter 14, "Rise and let go," are problematic texts.

Perhaps this text comes from a previous reflection about Galilee that has been omitted. We know from the Synoptic Gospels that Jesus was rejected in his home synagogue of Nazareth (cf. Matt 13:57, Mark 6:4, Luke 4:24). Is that why he says the Galileans who welcomed him had been at the feast in Jerusalem and had seen what he did there (4:45)? Are there two perspectives in Galilee about Jesus? There certainly were two perspectives about him in Jerusalem! And where is the "home area" for Jesus in this Johannine gospel? Is it Nazareth or Bethlehem? Or is this verse a proleptic warning that in the next cycle the rejection is coming? Does this verse then echo the perspective in the prologue where the evangelist tells us clearly that his own people rejected him (cf. 1:11)? It certainly stands in sharp contrast to the Samaritans who had just confessed Jesus to be the "Savior of the world" (4:42).[50] This issue is complex because of its brevity, but it leads us directly to the next story and beyond where conflict with Jesus will become more visible.

This story, however, opens with a reminder that we have come full circle and arrived back in Cana where Jesus transformed the water into wine (4:46; cf. 2:1). In this second Cana story an unnamed royal official (*basilikos*: proba- bly in the service of Herod Antipas) is our primary focus. He hails from the border town and tax-collecting center of Capernaum that lies nearly 600 feet below sea level. He apparently has heard of Jesus' arrival in the hill country of Cana high above the harp-shaped lake. When we meet this official, he has ascended the steep hills and is begging Jesus to come down to his home and heal his dying son (4:47).

Whether Jesus is exhausted or exasperated with the demands of the crowd or with this official we do not know, but he clearly voices a sense of frustra- tion when he tells the official "unless you see signs and wonders, you will not believe" (4:48). While readers of this story understand that the warning against wanting signs and wonders is also directed to them, the officer here does not respond directly to Jesus' statement. But it is not difficult to visualize that almost in panic, he must then plead for Jesus to "come down before my child dies!" The desperate plea of the caring father evidently moves Jesus deeply because he seems to respond quickly: "Go; your son will live" (4:48-50).

This story is a brief encapsulation of a very traumatic experience, and the Johannine storyteller captures the remarkable response of the father: "The man believed the word [that] Jesus said to him—and he departed!" (4:50). That

---

50 This confession is a reminder of the earlier strategic confession of John the Baptizer that Jesus is the Lamb of God who takes away the sin of the world (1:29). The confession of Jesus as "Savior" is used only once in this gospel and once in the Epistles of John (1 John 4:14). It is used in reference to God in Luke 1:47, three times in both 1 Timothy and Titus and in Jude 25. It is used elsewhere of Jesus in Luke (2:11) and Acts (5:3;1, 13:23), six times in the Pauline epistles, and five times in 2 Peter. It may reflect a warrior perspective of God as Savior in the Old Testament (cf. Ps 24:5 and Isa 12:2; 43:3, 11; 63:8).

response is nearly incredible. How many of us would have responded likewise if our child was dying? Yet, there is more to the story. As the officer walks down the deep valley incline back to Capernaum, his servants bring the message to him that his son is "living!" He quickly discovers that the healing occurred when Jesus said the boy would live (4:51-53). Then the evangelist tells us that the man and his family believe (4:53). But did you notice that he is said to believe twice? The impact is significant—if not a bit puzzling.

The issue of believing is an important theme in the Gospel of John. In fact, it is one of the primary concerns of the evangelist and is even a focus of the purpose statement (20:31). But I would remind you that believing is not mainly about affirming a set of propositions; it is about trusting in God and in God's Son, Jesus, who is the true embodiment of trust or believing the one true God when he visited the world as a human for a very short time. Indeed, he left an indelible impact on the people here, and he even created a body of believers who are to embody the characteristics of their Lord. This story of an official is a prime example of a person who embodied such believing so that when Jesus told him that his son would live, he took Jesus at his word and acted accordingly—though it might have seemed foolish to many observers that Jesus could heal someone at a distance.

This story mirrors the "faith" (*pistis*) of the Roman centurion whose servant was dying (Matt 8:5-10, Luke 7:1-10). Unlike most of the other writers of the New Testament, however, the Johannine evangelist does not use the Greek noun "faith." John uses only the verb "to believe" (*pisteuein*): by the time he wrote his gospel, people were already focusing too much on the content of what one believes and not on the relationship with the God in whom one believes.

The story of Jesus healing the official's son from a distance (and the Cana Cycle) ends with the evangelist calling the reader's attention to the fact that this story involves the "second sign" Jesus did. Now while some Christians may enjoy spending their spare time discussing issues such as the number of signs present in this gospel—with the hope of coming up with some special number (perhaps seven?)—the Johannine storyteller only counts to two! Then, he notes in his purpose statement that Jesus did "many other signs" (20:30). Perhaps those who focus on activities such as determining the number of signs Jesus did would be better served by answering the question: To what aspects of Jesus' life and ministry are those signs pointing? So, with these concluding comments, we close the Cana Cycle and its emphasis on believing. We turn next to consider the Festival Cycle and its disturbing emphasis on conflict.

Chapter 3

Stories of Conflict and the Festival Cycle
(5:1–11:57)

One of the most significant and enduring features of Israel's faith is the Jewish festival calendar established by God with Moses in the wilderness. Its purpose was to remind people to honor and celebrate God's special acts in creation and in liberating them from slavery in Egypt during the exodus experience. It was later expanded to imply additional meanings and to include other significant festival times when God's people recognized that God intervened to preserve Israel.

While there are other minor celebrated days in the Jewish calendar, there are basically four major Mosaic feasts designated (see Leviticus 23):

1. Sabbath (*shabb'ot*)
2. Passover (*Pesach*), or Unleavened Bread: in the first month, Nisan 14, 15–21
3. Pentecost (*Shavu'ot*), or the Feast of Weeks: fifty days after Nisan 15 in the month of Sivan
4. Tabernacles (*Sukk'ot*), or Booths (*Tishri* 15–22), which is included in the festive New Year (*Rosh Hoshannh, Tishri* 1–20) and the Holy Day of Atonement (*Yom Kippur, Tishri* 10)

In addition, there are two later feasts: 1. Dedication (*Hanukkah*): in the tenth month, or *Kislev* 25; added in the time of Judas Maccabeus and the defeat of the Syrians and 2. Feast of Purim: in the twelfth month of *Adar* (13–15); added in the time of Queen Esther.

A Sabbath Healing at Bethesda and the Charge of Blasphemy
(5:1-47)

With the above summary of the Jewish festival calendar in mind, I return to the Gospel of John and how the evangelist relates the conflicts of Jesus to several of those festivals.

[I would pause here briefly to remind my readers that it was because of the confusing organization of commentaries on these chapters and particularly because of Rudolf Bultmann's strange displacement of John 5 that originally led me into a restudy of the Jewish calendar. Innately I knew that the story in chapter 5 was about Sabbath, but I remain deeply indebted to my former colleagues in Old Testament, especially the late Marvin E. Tate and John D. W. Watts, among other former colleagues in Louisville, who helped me clarify my thinking on how the calendar was related to Sabbath.[51]]

The fascinating story in John 5 of a pathetic paralyzed man begins with a reference to an unnamed "feast of the Jews." Bultmann thought it was Pentecost, but anyone who is familiar with Leviticus 23 knows that the festival calendar begins with Sabbath. Moreover, every festival is really treated as a holy or solemn convocation to the Lord. So, if we are talking about festivals, one would expect us to begin our discussion by dealing with Sabbath—and that is exactly the focus of John 5.

The paralytic in our story has been suffering for about thirty-eight years and confined to the environs of the destitute at Bethesda, the site of five porches, just north of the Temple area.[52] When Jesus approaches the man and asks, "Do you want to get well?" the only response that comes to the man's mind is a complaint and a reference to a mythical view that an angel would periodically disturb the water and the first one who could get into the pool would be healed. Then like a frustrated invalid, he begins the blame game—namely, that he has no assistant to help him beat the others who are waiting for such an opportune moment.

(We now know that the man's sense that the waters were periodically disturbed was quite correct: Under the ancient pools at Bethesda there are holes in the rocky pits or caves where the water would collect and when these underground caves would fill with water, a syphon action would take place and water would gush out. But the man's rationale that an angel was the cause of the disturbance was completely fallacious, and the later emendation of the

---

51 See my introduction to the Festival Cycle in G. Borchert, *John 1–11*, 224–28 and 230, note 17. See Bultmann, *Gospel of John*, 237–46.

52 There are several alternate readings in various texts but Bethesda, located today near the Church of St. Anne in Jerusalem, seems the most logical. For a discussion of the site, see J. Jeremias, *The Rediscovery of Bethesda* (Louisville: SBTS, 1966).

text by an unknown scribe concerning such an angelic disturbance that was included in the King James version of the Bible (5:8) is unfortunate.[53])

Jesus, however, does not attempt to explain that God does not operate on a first-come basis. He simply says to the man: "Get up! Take your bedroll and walk" (5:8). The man does just that! Then we read the ominous words that it is "the Sabbath."[54]

The Jewish religious security agents are out doing their work, so they confront the healed man with his "unlawful" activity. In self-defense, the former paralytic complains that it is not his fault; that the fellow who healed him should be blamed. The paralytic does not know the name of his healer, but later finds the man: It is Jesus, who had warned the man to be careful and "Sin no more!" Then the man reports Jesus to the authorities (5:8-15), and his report leads the Jewish authorities to switch their attention from the healed man to Jesus and the opening of the controversy texts in this gospel. So, the storyteller indicates that the report is the initial reason why the Jews persecute Jesus—because he healed on the Sabbath (5:16).[55]

In his response to the inquisitors' claims, however, Jesus tells them that both he and his Father work on the Sabbath. That new claim is incredible for those agents of legalism, and they are prepared to eliminate Jesus from their sphere of influence by raising the charge to blasphemy—since he identified himself with God (5:17-18).

But the storyteller makes it clear that Jesus is not intimidated by his inquisitors. Rather, like a competent attorney in court, Jesus sets out his case by starting with a double "truly" statement (amēn, amēn) that serves as the equivalent of an oath. Then he indicates that the Son does not operate on his own authority. Instead, he follows the Father's lead in all prescribed patterns, including such crucial matters as life and death (5:19-21). Indeed, Jesus adds that the Father has given the role of judgment to the Son for the

---

53 This mythical explanation from a late manuscript was unfortunately included in the Greek edition of the text by Erasmus under threat of excommunication that was used by the translators of the KJV. In the later edition of the Greek text after the Reformation, however, it was removed when the threat was no longer a concern for the editor.

54 Sabbath for the rabbis was so significant that they devoted an entire section of the Mishnah to rules concerning Sabbath. See *The Mishnah*, trans. H. Danby (London: Oxford University Press, 1933), 100–121.

55 For an interpretation of these verses by a Sabbatarian, see Samuel Bacchiocchi, "John 5:17: Negation or Clarification of the Sabbath?" *AUSS* 19 (1981):3–19. See also G. Borchert, *John 1–11*, 235.

purpose of honoring the Son. Then, with another oath-like retort, Jesus asserts that believing in him is the basis for eternal life and the means for avoiding condemnation (5:24).

Yet to make sure the reader does not think that this discussion is purely of mortal consequence, the story shifts slightly, and one has the impression that Jesus is briefly portrayed as less of a defense attorney and more like the judge. And he informs those inquisitors that understanding the reality of the Son of God has eternal implications. Beginning with another oath-like statement (*amēn, amēn*), Jesus declares that the decisive "hour" is coming and indeed has arrived when the dead "will hear the voice of the Son of God and ... will live."[56]

Does it sound like the arrival of the *eschaton* (the end of time)? Indeed, it feels as though the Johannine evangelist is now writing as if he is the seer of the book of Revelation where Jesus, the Son of Man, is likened to the apocalyptic cloud-rider (5:27; cf. Rev 1:13, 14:14; Dan 7:13). Clearly, here he has been given authority from the Father to decide the fate of the good who will participate in the "resurrection of life" and of the evil who will be condemned to the "resurrection of judgment" (John 5:22-24). In our contemporary context where discussions of evil and condemnation are often politely avoided, these words of judgment in John are frequently trimmed from our hearing—or at least from recognizing that they could apply to us. But evil is a reality, and divine condemnation cannot be conveniently deleted from life as we might do with the touch of a button on our computers. Both evil and righteous judgment must be taken seriously.

Then having completed his brief excursus into the assigned role of Jesus in the eschaton, the Johannine storyteller returns to his earlier argument for the purpose of assuring his readers that the role of Jesus as the personal agent of God is powerfully confirmed by sufficient witnesses that the charge of blasphemy should be summarily dismissed.

To support his defense, Jesus argues that if he is alone in testifying to his authority and has no support that he was sent by God, then the charge

---

56 I would repeat what I indicated in my commentary: To understand eschatological statements concerning now and the ultimate future, the symbolism of Oscar Cullmann's illustrations of D-Day and V-Day from World War II can be very helpful. D-Day was a decisive event that promised the end of the war, but the world had to wait for V-Day to rejoice in the victory. See Cullmann, *Christ and Time* (Philadelphia: Westminster, 1950), 82–85, 140–41. See also G. Borchert, *John, 1–11*, 240.

of blasphemy might be legitimate,[57] but such is not the case. So, like a good attorney, he calls his witnesses to the stand. John, the Baptizer, is the first witness he calls because even his critics have checked with John. Yet, Jesus further argues that he does not really need the testimony of mere mortals like John (5:33-35) because Jesus' own works give witness to God's presence and call on his life and actions (5:36). Of course, he could call the Father to witness (5:37), but his critics would not even recognize who the Father is and do not even believe in him (5:38) Next, Jesus firmly asserts that although those scholars have looked for evidence in the Scriptures concerning his coming and the gift of life, they have completely missed the point of their reading because their focus is on legalism and therefore they have completely been misdirected (5:39-44). But the clinching witness, Jesus declares, is Moses. Although they place their hope and trust in him and the Torah, it is Moses who proves that they do not believe. Instead, they will discover that it is Moses who will judge and condemn them for their failure to believe in Jesus (5:45-47). [58]

Accordingly, from the evangelist's viewpoint, the argument is decisive. All charges against Jesus should be dismissed. The case against Jesus violating the Sabbath must be closed!

So, we must move on to the next festival story—which involves Passover.

Passover, Two Signs, and the Reenactment of the Exodus Grumbling (6:1-71)

It would be virtually impossible to discuss the Jewish calendar without reference to the Passover, which could quite easily be designated as the birthday of the "people of Israel"—namely, a distinct group or nation, although it had been in quest of a homeland. Intimately associated with this initial event of Passover (the death of the firstborn of Egypt and the "passing over" of the firstborn of Israel by the death angel) is Israel's escape from slavery in Egypt. This escape involved God's control over the waters of the Red Sea (or Sea of Reeds) and God's providing the people with food for their forty-year journey through the wilderness to the promised land. It is hardly a surprise then that the Johannine storyteller links the two major miracle stories involving water and food from

---

57 See *Mishnah*, Ketub. 2.9

58 For my further explication of these arguments in John 5:31-47, see G. Borchert, *John 1–11*, 243–49.

the life of Jesus (found in all four gospels) with the festival of Passover (6:4).[59] The story of John 6 unites the powerful story of Israel's beginning with the incomparable story of the incarnate ministry of Jesus.

This second story in the Johannine Festival Cycle moves the attention of readers from Jerusalem to the north near the shores of the harp-shaped Sea of Galilee, which in Roman times was also known as the Sea of Tiberias (6:1).

[I should note here again that while contemporary Western readers may be committed to their understanding of chronological and geographical order, they should not criticize the Johannine evangelist's order of events because his purpose is not chronology or geography: another emphasis drives his arrangement and selection of the stories. This difference has often led even some of our leading commentators on the gospel to posit a rearrangement of the chapters.]

This story begins with Jesus and the disciples in the hills above the nearby lake and Jesus pointing out that a large crowd is attempting to follow them because the people have seen the signs he is doing (6:2). As the story continues, the evangelist tells us that Jesus tests Philip by asking him how much it would cost to feed the crowd (6:5). The disciple's response is basically that such an idea is foolish because it would take more than half a year's wages of a laborer (200 denarii) to provide even a small morsel for everyone (6:7). But Andrew, who often tries to help in tense situations, finds a lad with a lunch of five loaves and two fish. Yet the general reaction is that the meager resource is virtually nothing for such a large crowd. The situation seems hopeless.

Jesus, however, tells the disciples to have the people sit down on the grass. (Mark 6:40 adds that they were seated in groups of hundreds and fifties). The estimated size of the crowd is about five thousand men ("besides women and children," cf. Matt 14:21).[60] After giving thanks (*eucharistēsas*), Jesus distributes the loaves and fish so that the people have as much to eat as they wish (John 6:11). And when they are filled, Jesus instructs the disciples to gather the remainder: they return with an amazing twelve baskets of fragments (6:12).

This story is so well known that for many people it may hardly cause much more than a yawn. And that may be because of the matter-of-fact way

---

59 I am quite aware of the similarities in some healing stories and between the large catch of fish in the resurrection story of John 21 and the call of the disciples in Luke 5, but they do not alter my statement.

60 While I am not a scholar who spends his time attempting to harmonize the gospel accounts to eliminate differences in the various gospel stories, these additions seem quite likely.

that John tells the story. This sign event and the one that follows, however, are in fact shocking, but they serve as the framework for implications far beyond them. Clearly, they provide a basis for showing how John sees Passover and the Exodus impacting his understanding of Jesus. Now, do not think that I am suggesting the Johannine evangelist is uninterested in the miraculous: one of the major themes in the gospel involves the "signs" Jesus did (cf. 20:30). But signs in this gospel are not ends in themselves; they are pointers to who Jesus is and the nature of his mission. Both God and Jesus can and did indeed control the water: just as God fed the children of Israel for forty years in the desert, so Jesus fed more than five thousand people in a single event.

Miracle stories such as those detailed here seldom occur today. Accordingly, I have asked myself: Why is the reaction of many Christians not amazement? Do we think that such actions cannot take place with God? Are they just old stories that we do not take seriously? I trust that such is not the case. Yet, rereading these stories has forced me to reexamine my own reactions. Were there actually twelve baskets of fragments, or is that number just a convenient biblical symbol—a designation for the completeness of the people of God or the church? The number twelve certainly has symbolic implications through the history of Christian interpretation and of both covenant periods. But I have wondered if these miracles happened today, would we be ready to proclaim, "This is indeed the prophet who is to come into the world" (6:14)?

In the story of the feeding of the large crowd, the people who experience this miracle, which the storyteller labels as a "sign" (6:14), are so amazed that they are ready to make Jesus their king—by force if necessary! But the goal of Jesus is not to become a kingly ruler, as we discover in the synoptic temptation stories (cf. Matt 4:8-10, Luke 4:5-8). So, faced with such public pressure in this story, Jesus simply withdraws to the hills to be by himself (John 6:15).

But being in the hills provides the Johannine storyteller with the context for the next segment of his story. It begins with the disciples leaving the far side of the lake (the eastern area today near the Jordanian highlands) and their intent on crossing over to the north side near Capernaum (6:16). But in a typical feature of the area, a strong wind barrels down the valley of pigeons/doves and hits the lake with a fierce storm. Yet in a Johannine understatement of a crisis, Jesus comes calmly walking on the water. When the disciples see this figure coming toward them, they are terrified. But Jesus seeks to calm their fears by employing the familiar Johannine expression "I am!" (*egō eimi*),[61] and adding "Do not be afraid" (6:20). With joy they then welcome him into the boat, and they "immediately" arrive at their destination. When one compares this Johannine account with those in the Synoptic Gospels, one has the distinct feeling that John has purposely played down the emotional impact of these events: the evangelist probably is focused on the "Exodus implications" and the further interpretation of these signs.

After a few linking sentences, the evangelist takes the people to Capernaum where Jesus has already come. The storyteller then is ready to continue his narrative. Yet the conversation soon becomes more heated and reminds the reader of being in a synagogue dispute rather than in a conversation with random followers of Jesus. This contextual change to a dispute is later confirmed by the evangelist at the end of the dialogue (6:59).

The people soon begin asking questions about when Jesus arrived, since they did not see him leaving in a boat. But Jesus does not focus on such a pedantic discussion. Instead, they open the conversation by indicating that they are *not* seeking his "signs," but they are more interested in the bread he supplied them. (Unfortunately, in the history of the transmission of the text, at John 6:26 the King James Version makes a strategic error by using the word "miracles" instead of "signs.") The people are in fact seeking more miracles. Indeed, they have ingested the miracle of the bread and want more, but they have missed the "sign" in the miracle. For that reason, Jesus says "Don't work for food that perishes." So, he counters that their goal should be working for food that brings "eternal life," which is the gift of the "Son of Man"—the one who has the seal of God (6:27).

As we might expect, the people hear only part of his message—the part about their working for God and not about the Son's gift to them. So, Jesus has to clarify that their work is to believe in the one whom God sent (6:29). That kind of work does not interest them, however. Instead, they counter by asking Jesus for a "sign" as the basis for their believing—namely, what work he is doing (6:30). Then they imply that they understand the way of God and that in the wilderness God gave "bread from heaven" to their ancestors (6:31). It is as if they are toying with Jesus. So, in responding to their reply, Jesus

---

61 It is interesting that this story is one of the few places that the Synoptics use the expression "*egō eimi.*" It can simply mean "It is I," but for John, the meaning has important theological consequences. Perhaps that is the reason so many translators use a more usual translation at this point in John.

uses a double "*amēn*" oath-like response and reminds them that it was not Moses who gave them the bread but "my Father" who is the supplier of bread "from heaven" that provides "life for the world" (6:32-33). When the people hear that response, they think Jesus is offering them a sustaining solution to their human need for food, and they ask for that bread (6:34)—much like the woman of Samaria wants the bubbling water of Jesus.

But they hardly anticipate that his response would be that he is the "bread of life"[62] and that for those who believe in him, he would supply their hunger and thirst (6:35). Jesus understands that they do not believe, yet his invitation is that he would not turn away those whom the Father gives him. In coming to the world, the goal of Jesus always has been to do the will of the one who sent him and to lose none of them. Indeed, the will of the Father[63] is that "everyone who sees the Son and believes in him should have eternal life." Moreover, the clear goal of Jesus is to "raise up [all those who believe] at the last day" (6:36-40).

In case you have not anticipated the people "grumbling," as they did in the wilderness, the evangelist confirms that Jesus soon encounters a repeat of that earlier response (6:41). They think that his claim of coming down from heaven is outlandish! (I suspect that if we heard such a claim today, we would insist that such a person should see a psychiatrist.) So, they ask the natural questions: Is he not "the son of Joseph?" Don't we know his parents (6:42)?

(Do you think the people's grumbling was unreasonable? Would you have responded differently? I have often wondered what was going on in the mind of Jesus during this exchange. Was he surprised? He certainly tried to calm the people's anxiety by telling them that they did not need to grumble. He clearly must have sensed that the confrontations were growing and that reasoning with such strident opponents would not be very productive. But even though he tried, he must have known that the situation was on a downward trajectory.)

Jesus reminds those who earlier wanted to make him their king that God is still in change and knows those who would be drawn to Jesus and would

---

62 Prior to this point in John, the expression *egō eimi* ("I am") has not been used with a predicate nominative to complete the sentence. Here it is so used as "I am the bread of life." Henceforth it will be used both ways, but in the expanded form it will be with predicates such as: "vine," "door," "good shepherd," "the resurrection and the life," "the way, the truth and the life," etc.

63 As you read this gospel and note the high Christology that is espoused, do not overlook the fact that the gospel remains unapologetically theocentric. Jesus consistently insists throughout the arguments that he is being subject to the will of the Father.

experience the resurrection (6:44). Indeed, he reminds his opponents that the prophets had predicted God would teach people to understand God's ways and such people would come to him (6:45).

Then, drawing the dispute to a climax and using another oath-like (*amēn, amēn*) saying, Jesus firmly informs them: "I am the bread of life" and that their ancestors "ate manna in the wilderness, and they died!" But that is not the way it is with "the living bread who came down from heaven." The one eating this bread—"my flesh"—"will live forever" (6:47-51). The mention of eating his flesh must have sounded like cannibalism to the Jews who were listening. (I would remind you that in the early centuries of the church, those who misunderstood the symbolic celebrative nature of the Lord's Supper or Eucharist often charged Christians with advocating cannibalism.[64])

But the Johannine evangelist does not seek to soften the statement. Instead, Jesus makes the statement more intense with another double "*amēn*" oath-like saying when he forthrightly asserts that those who fail to "eat the flesh of the Son of man and drink his blood" would "have no life" in them. Indeed, he even adds that "my flesh is truly food ... and my blood is truly drink" (6:53-55).

Jesus could not have been more assertive. But he then calls the Father to witness that "he who eats me will live forever" (6:57-59). Jesus does not soft-pedal his testimony. If you were in the synagogue at this point and were being addressed so forcefully, you would probably realize that you had only two possible reactions (6:59): agree with Jesus or be hostile to the point of being livid. In this situation Jesus is hardly the sweet, mild-mannered Christ who is often painted by humans: he is much more like the "lion" Jesus in the Book of Revelation.

Now do not think for a moment that this discussion has no impact on those who are following Jesus: the storyteller makes it clear that "many disciples" found the claims of Jesus to be very hard to accept (6:60). Indeed, it is as though Jesus has crossed his Rubicon and is unwilling to turn back. He even probes them further by asking them to consider the possibility of him

---

64 The Jews regarded eating flesh and drinking blood as an intolerable thought. It was practiced among some Gentiles in ritual services such as with the Pythion priestesses, but this type of practice was strictly forbidden for the Jews. See Gen 9:4-7, Lev 17:10-14, and Deut 12:16. For further insights on this issue of viewing the Lord's Supper or Eucharist as eating and drinking the body and blood of Christ, see Craig Koester's helpful work on *Symbolism in the Fourth Gospel* (Minneapolis: Fortress, 1995), 95–100.

being the eschatological Son of Man, and able to reenter the heavenly realm (6:61-62). And he challenges them to be clear on the difference between the reality of the life-giving spirit and the way of the flesh. He is completely aware of those who believe and are drawn to him by the Father, and of those who do not believe. He is not confused: he even knows who will betray him (6:63-65).

At this point the storyteller informs us that many disciples no longer follow Jesus (6:66). Then Jesus questions his intimate disciples about whether they will also leave him. Peter responds for the twelve with a question ("Lord, to whom shall we go?") and a confession ("You have the words of eternal life! We have believed and we know that you are the Holy One of God!"). It is one of the great confessions in the Fourth Gospel (6:68-69; cf. 1:29, 4:42). But do not forget the context of hostility in which it is given.

That context is also one of the extreme pathos as Jesus apparently verbalizes his thoughts that he had chosen "twelve, and one of you is a devil." The text here in fact names the "devil-man" as Judas, the son of Iscariot, as the one who will betray him (6:70-71).

While Jesus apparently knew the identify of his betrayer, I wonder how much he told the disciples, since they did not seem to know too much at the final supper (13:21-26). But for John and for the Christian Church, Judas Iscariot continues to bear the designation of the "devil-man." He should never be viewed simply as a tragic, mistaken figure as is portrayed in the musical, *Jesus Christ Superstar*. We will meet him again as a thief and a betrayer, but the storyteller offers Judas no reprieve from his evil. He remains a devil and a warning to all those who would be tempted to exchange personal integrity for the world's acceptance and its benefits. His master is the devil, the one who weaves enticing webs to entangle and trap unsuspecting humans in his deceptive goals.

With this sobering conclusion, we turn from the Passover and the Exodus in the story to the Festival of Tabernacles and the growing hostility between the Jewish authorities and Jesus.

Tabernacles and the Face-off over Freedom
(7:1–9:41)

In developing his crisis-filled narrative, the Johannine storyteller moves from the historic celebration of Passover in chapter 6 to the most festive month of Tishri and the celebration of *Sukkot* (Tabernacles or Booths) but with a continuing emphasis on the ancient story of the Exodus. Note here that while some commentators have recognized the close connection of chapters 7 and 8, I am convinced that this section also includes the story of the blind man in chapter 9.[65]

Five days after *Yom Kippur* (Atonement), the feast of Tabernacles begins. Many Jews in the time of Jesus, especially farmers and other rural people, would have packed their tents or temporary sleeping arrangements and headed for the festivities in Jerusalem. Some years, however, they would celebrate this festival at an alternative place of enjoyment and relaxation. Wherever the particular holiday period in John is held, the farming community is ready for "R and R" in this month of *Tishri*.

Farmers have brought in the harvest, so Jerusalem and the other places are made ready for a celebration. Indeed, even the brothers of Jesus (who did not believe in him; cf. 7:5) are aware that, if he wants attention, the time of "Booths" would be the best period to announce his "messiahship." But the Johannine storyteller knows that the brothers have the wrong perspective on Jesus and Tabernacles. Therefore, he introduces this story with the note that the Jews want to kill (*apokteinai*) Jesus, so he is staying in Galilee (7:1).

Nevertheless, several days later Jesus also goes to the temple—not for a "holiday" or for proclaiming himself to be the Messiah, but for the purpose of teaching (7:14). His presence, however, immediately raises questions in the minds of those in Jerusalem—such as how he received his learning since he has not been to a rabbinic school.[66] The response of Jesus, therefore, is to claim an education from the one who sent him and to charge his inquirers with breaking the law of Moses (7:16-19).

The face-off with the crowd (*ochlos*) is almost immediate as they charge Jesus with having a demon, but he responds that they are confused about the crucial issues of circumcision and Sabbath: Whereas they circumcise on the Sabbath, he heals the whole body on the Sabbath. In other words, Jesus is saying that in their pedantic casuistic arguments and exception clauses they

---

65 See G. Borchert, *John 1–11*, 277–280. Contrast, e.g., the views of George R. Beasley-Murray, *John*, in vol. 36, *Word Biblical Commentary* (Waco, TX: Word, 1987), 104 and D.A. Carson, *The Gospel According to John* (Grand Rapids: Eerdmans, 1991), 304–05.
66 The rabbis and leadership of the Jews considered most of the working class (the *am haeretz*) to be uneducated (cf. Acts 4:13).

are completely confused (7:20-24).[67] The crowd counters with issues such as: why the authorities are seeking to kill him, the nature of who Christ might be, and the significance of the signs he is doing. Even though the leadership try to arrest him, they are unable to do so because "his hour had not yet come." So, the confusion continues (7:25-31). Then, when the authorities send their henchmen to arrest Jesus, he tells them that he will only be with them a little longer and they cannot come where he is going. In surprise, they wonder if he is going to the Diaspora of the Jews (7:32-36). [68]

Then, on the last day of the feast —"the Great Day" (7:37-38)—the Pharisees particularly emphasize their prayers for rain because in their urban settings their cisterns are usually almost dry by *Tishri* (our September). Jesus takes the opportunity to announce his gift of "rivers of living water." (At the time John was writing this story, the Sadducean fierce opposition to this rain prayer had virtually been eliminated. Those defenders of the Temple had basically disappeared after the Temple's destruction in AD/CE 70.[69] Accordingly, the term "Sadducees" does not appear in John's gospel.) The storyteller knows he is living in a post-Temple, post-Sadducean era when the coming of "living water" is identified with the new era and with the gift of the Spirit and the glorification of Jesus (7:39). Indeed, John wants his readers to know that Jesus is a convincing teacher and that many people have wrestled with and been generally accepting of his teaching (7:40).

So, the storyteller quickly returns to the conflict and the confusion among the people and their debate about whether Jesus might be the expected prophet, the Christ, or might be from Bethlehem, the hometown of David. When the officers, therefore, return to the council without making an arrest, the authorities are frustrated and angry because they judge that even their officers/guards are as legally incompetent as the people because they have listened to the crowd that lacks religious understanding (7:44-49). Or did they?

---

67 It was a casuistic argument based on their exception clauses. They did have an exception for limited healing in the cases that could be interpreted as the potential of immanent death (t. *Sabb.*5.16, *Yoma* 85, *Mek.* 31.13), but they later removed even those exceptions. See Str-B 2.478.

68 These were Jews who lived in lands beyond Palestine.

69 For a discussion concerning the Sadducean high priest's (Alexander Jannaeus') desecration of the rain festival and the killing of the Pharisees in the Temple complex after the Pharisees pelted him with citrons, see G. Borchert, *John 1–11*, 288–91 and the accompanying footnotes. See also Gerald L. Borchert, *Jesus of Nazareth: Background, Witnesses and Significance* (Macon, GA: Mercer University Press, 2011), 19 –22, 59–65.

At this point, Nicodemus (the Pharisee, who earlier had visited Jesus at night) speaks up in the council (the Jewish Sanhedrin) and asks if it is fair to judge a person without hearing from him. Probably out of sheer exasperation, his legalistic colleagues on the council slough off his question with a dismissive question of their own by asking if he is also one of those unbeknown Jews who comes from the Gentile territory of Galilee. They have already reached a decision about this Jesus: they are sure "no prophet is to rise from Galilee" (7:52; cf. Matt 4:15-16).

With this obvious indication that the Sanhedrin is a biased court/council in its perspectives, the evangelist shifts his attention to a different historical aspect of the Exodus—namely, that God is light and had led the people of Israel during their wilderness night travels by means of a pillar of fire/light. Accordingly, Jesus here identifies himself with another *egō eimi* ("I am") saying as the "light of the world" and that those who follow him will not walk in darkness (8:12; cf. Exod 13:21).

[Before I delve more fully into this discussion of light and freedom and Jesus as the authentic witness to the truth, I must pause and comment briefly on the text of John 7:53–8:1, (frequently known as the *pericope de adultura/ adulteress*). While I believe it should be treated as an authentic story from the life of Jesus, I seriously doubt that it belongs at this point in the text or that it was even written by the Johannine evangelist. Our oldest Greek manuscripts of John do not include this text, and it is missing from the early Syriac and Coptic versions. It can be found in some Western Greek texts from the fourth/fifth centuries (for example, Codex Bezae) and later Western Greek and Latin manuscripts, but not in any major early Eastern Greek manuscripts. It is similar to a story from Luke rather than from the writings of John, and it does appear in some later Greek manuscripts after Luke 21:25 and in several other places in John 7 and after John 21:25. I do consider that it should be treated as a legitimate canonical text, but not from John. It is more like a text looking for a context. I should also mention that the story includes the Greek word for "scribes," *grammateis* (8:3), which is found nowhere else in John. If you are interested in my further comments concerning this reminiscence from the life of Jesus, please see my extended commentary and footnotes there on these verses.[70]]

---

70 See my commentary, "IV. A Biblical Addition: The Woman Seized in Adultery (*Pericope De Adultura* [7:53–8:11])" in G. Borchert, *John 1–11*, 369–76.

The announcement that Jesus is the "light of the world" initiates a new set of arguments between Jesus and the Pharisees in the Temple treasury (8:20). They charge Jesus with bearing witness to himself, and therefore his witness must be false (8:13). Jesus counters their charge with a further claim of their ignorance concerning from "whence he has come" and "whither he is going." In other words, they have no understanding concerning his mission and consequently they lack the basis for evaluating him. Clearly, they are unable to comprehend his testimony or that of his Father (8:14-18). When they demand to hear from the Father, Jesus informs them that they are ignorant of both him and his Father. But they cannot arrest him because, the evangelist interjects, his "hour" has not yet come (8:20).

The hint of the "hour," however, leads Jesus to shift the conversation again: he tells the people that he is going away but they cannot come. They respond by asking if he will kill himself. Jesus answers their foolish question by saying "You are from below; I am from above." They are simply tied to this world. The point is that they will die in their sins unless they believe that he is the "I am" (*ego eimi*; 8:24)! They end with the obvious question, "Who are you?" (8:25). Even though Jesus has told them from the beginning, the conversation is beyond their comprehension. They are stuck in the concerns of the world and do not understand his messages about himself or the Father. So, he counters with "When you have lifted up the Son of Man," you will know that Jesus is the "1 am" (*ege eimi*, 8:28). "I do nothing on my own, but only what the Father taught me." And the evangelist adds that many people come to believe even as he is speaking (8:30).

Jesus then addresses those Jews who are believing in him: "If you remain committed to my word, you will know the truth and the truth will set you free" (8:32). But such an idea is too much for them, for they rely on their Abrahamic heritage for their security. Accordingly, they advise Jesus that they have never been in bondage to anyone: How could they be made free? (8:33). That response is an historical falsehood concerning the people of Israel, but they consider themselves to be free to follow the law. So, Jesus answers them on their terms: They are slaves of sin and need the "Son" to set them free. They claim Abraham as their father, but they are seeking to kill Jesus— Abraham would never do such a thing (8:40)! The conversation moves in a fast, downward spiral. Then Jesus states that they follow the practices of their father. When they contradict Jesus, he tells them point blank that their father is the devil, and they are following his wishes because his nature is both murdering and lying and there is no truth in him (8:44).

Although some of the Jews had indicated earlier that they believed him, they really did not. Jesus has obviously demonstrated their lack of believing. Then he advises them that they refuse to believe because they are not from God (8:47), leading them to call him one of the worst names that probably could come to their minds: He must be a Samaritan and have a demon! In a society where shame and honor are crucial categories of life, they try their best to dishonor him. But he responds with another double *amēn* oath-like statement saying: "If anyone keeps my word, he will never see death." That statement is again too much for them. They are quite certain that Jesus must have a demon because Abraham and the prophets are all dead. So, they challenge Jesus: "Are you greater than Father Abraham—who died?" And what about the prophets? They throw down their gauntlet, but Jesus picks it up and answers that he is not in the business of self-glorification: glorification is God's business. They do not know God, but "I know him and keep his word." Moreover, "Abraham rejoiced ... to see my day" (8:56).

How do you react to Jesus' answer? His statement is beyond reason for his challengers. Jesus is not even fifty years old, but he is proclaiming that he has seen Abraham. How is that idea even plausible? But they certainly do not know Jesus, and he asserts with another oath-like statement: "Before Abraham came to be, 'I am!'" (*egō eimi*; 8:58). His challengers are ready to stone Jesus, but he vanishes and departs the Temple. So, we must turn to the next story in this face-off.

The final story in this three-chapter episode brings us back to Jesus, the light of the world (9:5) and the further revelation of Jesus as God's messenger. The story involves a man who has been blind from birth, and the issue concerns the historic question of theodicy that has vexed humans for millennia.[71] The disciples have their pet questions for Jesus, and they are ready to probe whether it is the blind man or his parents who are to blame for his condition. When Jesus tells them they are asking the wrong question, they are scarcely ready for the story that follows. Indeed, few are ready for the work that Jesus is about to do—certainly not the Pharisees. When Jesus again announces that he is the light of the world, little does anyone expect him to give the blind man sight.

---

71 See my discussion on the questions of evil, suffering, theodicy, and dealing with the Dark Side in Gerald L. Borchert, *Tension*, 17–31. See also G. Gerstenberger and W. Schrage, *Suffering* (Nashville: Abingdon, 1980), 229–31.

But that is what happens: Jesus makes mud from his spittle,[72] places it on the man's eyes, and sends him to the Pool of Siloam to wash.

For the first time in his life the man can see, although he does not know who healed him (9:1-7)! Then questions begin to swirl around him, especially after the Pharisees become involved. The healing occurred on the Sabbath! The religious investigators are again at work and seek the lawbreaker, but they do not make much headway. So, they check with the man's parents to determine if his healing is legitimate. The parents agree that their son had been born blind, but they do not want to get involved further and be censured.

When the Pharisees meet with the man again, since for them he is an obvious sinner, they instruct him to give thanks to God for the healing but that he should regard the healer as a sinner. The former blind man, however, does not understand their religious distinctions and responds that "Never before had a man who was born blind been healed. If the healer was not from God, he could do nothing" (9:24–33). The former blind man does not enter into the Pharisees' games with religious words and tells the Pharisees it is a marvel that they do not know the origin of the healer and yet he healed one born blind. That statement is too much for the investigators, and they condemn the man as being born in complete sinfulness. His attempt to teach the authorities about God is also more than they can stomach. So they promptly excommunicate the former blind man from the synagogue (9:34).

But that is not the end of the story. Jesus finds the man who has been condemned and asks him if he believes in the Son of Man. When the man asks Jesus who the healer was, Jesus tells him. The man immediately responds, "Lord, I believe," and he worships Jesus! [73]

This story climaxes with a magnificent summation by Jesus: "For judgment I came into the world that those who do not see may see and those who see may become blind." The ever-lurking Pharisees then come forward and ask Jesus if he is talking about them. (Perhaps Jesus answered: "Yes, if the shoe fits, then the condemning Pharisees should put it on!")

Have you ever wondered if some of those condemning Pharisees might still be lurking around our religious institutions today? Were they just stick

---

72 Compare also the two times in Mark that Jesus used spittle to heal persons: a deaf man with a speech problem (7:32-35) and a blind man (8:22-25).

73 Note the wordplay on *kurios/kyrios* between vv. 36 and 38. When the man asks Jesus who the healer is, the evangelist uses *kurie* as "sir." But once Jesus explains, then the evangelist uses *kurie* as a confession "Lord."

figures in our biblical stories, or could they be real living people today? With these questions, it is time to shift to the next chilling confrontation.

Winter, Dedication, and the First *Mashal*: The Shepherd and the Door (10:1-42)

We come now to the penultimate section of the Festival Cycle and to the introduction of the Feast of Dedication (*Hanukkah*) as the conflict between Jesus and the Jews continues to intensify. While some scholars are troubled by the multiple subjects in chapter 10 of John, I consider the structure to be a genuinely fascinating interweaving of themes concerning Jewish and Christian messianic thinking.[74]

But before I launch into this complex story, it is important that I make some brief comments concerning the two major parables or *mashalim* in John. For those who have focused their study of parables in the Synoptic Gospels and have learned from disciples of A. Jülicher that parables should have one main point, they may be a little confused by the Johannine parabolic stories in chapters 10 (the Good Shepherd) and 15 (the Vine and Branches). They may even call these parables "allegories."[75] But I would suggest that using the Hebrew term *mashal* or *mashalim* (pl.) may avoid that unnecessary limitation to our understanding. I would, therefore, suggest that one should use the texts of Ezekiel 34, Jeremiah 23, and Psalm 23 as more appropriate extended messianic shepherd texts for comparison with John 10.

In addition, I should add that the Johannine storyteller's choice of the Feast of Dedication provides an excellent background for introducing the Good Shepherd *mashal* and its emphasis on "lay[ing] down his life for the sheep" (10:15). This feast of Dedication picks up the emphasis of freedom from chapter 8 and is a memorial "to the rejection of false rulers and to the rededication of the Temple under Judas Maccabaeus."[76]

---

74 Several scholars find the interweaving here to be frustrating to their Western mindsets and propose numerous dislocations of the texts of John. The interesting example of one who finds dislocations in many texts but excludes chs. 9–12 is F.W. Lewis, *Disarrangements in the Fourth Gospel* (Cambridge: University Press. 1910).

75 For a helpful historical introduction to parables, see Criag Blomberg, *Interpreting the Parables* (Downers Grove: InterVarsity, 1990). See also Raymond Brown, "Parable and Allegory Reconsidered," Nov. T 5 (1962), 36–45.

76 See my further comments on this interconnection of messianic expectations and *Hanukkah* in G. Borchert, *John 1–11*, 327–29.

Now, for those of us who have spent most of our lives in the Western world where shepherding sheep is done with dogs, it may be difficult to envision the intimate relationship described in biblical passages that deal with a shepherd and his sheep. Having lived in Jerusalem and having spent time in areas where shepherds keep their sheep, I learned a great deal about how shepherds can mix their small herds and not be concerned with sheep getting confused about who is their shepherd: When the shepherd is ready to move out to pasture in the morning, he can call out his sheep from the mixed fold by singing or speaking—and only his own sheep will follow him. Those sheep know and understand his voice!

This phenomenal intimacy between shepherd and sheep was brought home to me when I looked out of the window of my tower bedroom one morning in Jerusalem and watched a shepherd leading his sheep past the Jaffa gate. Cars were whizzing by as the sheep nonchalantly followed their shepherd along the road, not troubled by all the noise of the city traffic. Sheep are smarter than we may think![77]

As we turn to discuss this complex *mashal*, I do not want you to become confused by the interweaving of the shepherd and the door in this first Johannine *mashal*. Many sheep pens or folds in Israel do not have doors or gates: the shepherd often serves at night as the door, lying across the opening at the front of the sheepfold. With this introduction in mind, we are ready to reflect on the fascinating parabolic story that John communicates to us about Jesus in chapter 10.

The account opens with another double *amēn*, an oath-like statement that signals to the reader that this story has serious implications. This impression is further highlighted by the fact that the enemy or attacker of the sheepfold is introduced before the shepherd. The warning has been sounded. The sheep are in danger. Pay attention! The gatekeeper knows the difference between the shepherd and strangers or thieves—and so do the sheep (10:1–5). Moreover, the storyteller indicates that Jesus uses this story pattern because his listeners are not understanding his message about the dangers they are facing (10:6).

Then in retelling this *mashal*, the storyteller shifts his focus on Jesus from the shepherd to the door or guardian of the sheepfold. He issues another double *amēn* assertion that reflects a stern reminder to his readers that all who came before him (Jesus) were thieves and robbers whose goal was to steal, kill, and

---

77 See my further account in G. Borchert, *John 1–11*, 330–31.

destroy the sheep (10:10; note the triad). The sheep, however, must not follow these strangers. Instead, the sheep have been given a gracious alternative. They can enter the sheepfold by the door (which is Jesus) and find pasture, safety, and life, because, as the "good" (*kalos*) shepherd, Jesus is the one who knows and cares for his sheep (10:7-11). Moreover, he is not a mere hired hand who cares little for the welfare of the sheep; nor is he one who would abandon the sheep when a wild wolf would stalk them, scatter them, and kill them. Jesus is the good shepherd who knows his sheep, and the sheep know him. Indeed, he "lays down his life for the sheep"—all his sheep (10:11-15, 17-18).

To know this self-giving Jesus is to know that his mission is expansive. It is hardly limited to a special in-group who are all from one nation, one culture, or one ethnicity. Exclusivity may be the way of humanity, but it is not the gospel! There is only one "flock" or "herd" (*poimnē*)[78] and one shepherd, and his mission has been to lay down his life for his sheep. That mission is like an echoing drumbeat that continues through this *mashal*. It is the mission of Jesus, the one who will lay down his life so that he can take it again—in the power of the resurrection. To be the shepherd of all is nothing less than his divine commission.

Not until the entire *mashal* is completed does the storyteller allow anything to interrupt the storyline. The shepherd is poised to lay down his life for his sheep, just as the Lamb of God will be sacrificed for the sin of the world (1:29). Do you sense the power of this story? Once again, the people are divided: some judge Jesus' claims to be demonic, while others wonder how a demon could open blind eyes.

But just then, the evangelist inserts a bell-tolling announcement: "It was the feast of Dedication—it was winter!"[79] That announcement is not a simple time-and-temperature statement; it is as though the story has stopped and the temperature plunged. The Jews are ready to pounce on Jesus, and they begin by telling him that they have had enough suspense. They want to know then and there: "Are you the Christ?" The response of Jesus is just as forthright:

---

78 The KJV renders this Greek word as one "fold," but it is better to render the term as "flock" or "herd"—which includes a number of sheep "pens" or "folds" of sheep. See G. Borchert, *John 1–11*, 334.

79 The celebration of *Hanukkah* or Dedication was celebrated as a memorial to cleansing and rededication of the Temple on the 25th of *Chislev* after Judas Maccabeus liberated the Jews from the Syrians who had defiled the Temple.

"I told you and you do not believe!" Then he reminds them that the works he has done are in the Father's name, but they do not believe.

Then the storyteller pictures Jesus as hammering the nails into the argument. First, he tells them that they are following their unbelieving leaders: therefore, they are not his sheep. Then, he indicates that they cannot even understand his argument (hear his voice). Thereafter, he says that he gives his sheep eternal life and that his sheep have security—which means his listeners do not. Then, he promises that his sheep also have security in the Father because he and the Father "are one" (10:27-30). It is hardly surprising that on hearing that fist-ful of condemnations that the people are prepared to stone Jesus (10:31).

[I pause here to address the issue of security. The perishing of Christ's sheep was likely not countenanced by most early Christians in the time of John unless it meant martyrdom, because they were living in an era of persecution when it could cost them their lives even to be Christians. But most contemporary Christians are not living in such a state. Could those early Christians turn away from their shepherd? Indeed, some did, as the elder John indicates in the First Epistle. And he condemned them. That is precisely the reason he wrote his magnificent theological warning not to copy those who deserted the community, but instead to copy the way of their Lord. Those Christians were not debating issues of "once saved." They were living with threats from those who hated them, as they hated their Lord (1 John 2:18-24; 3:9-10, 16-18; 4:1-4, 7-11; 5:4).]

In John's gospel when Jesus asks for which of his mighty works the people are planning to stone him, they parry his question with the charge of blasphemy. But Jesus defends his works, which should be sufficient to convince them that his works would clarify the authenticity of his words (10:32-39). Not having convinced them, though, Jesus departs and crosses to the other side of the Jordan River (where John had once been baptizing). A critical pause enters before the storyteller moves us to the climactic Lazarus story and the conclusion to the Festival Cycle.

The Climactic Story of Lazarus and the Fatal Decision
(11:1-57)

We come now to the climactic story of this second cycle that began with Sabbath and moved through a circle of feasts from Passover to Tabernacles and Dedication, and then we turn back to Passover (11:55) with the crucial story of Lazarus. The structure of this cycle thus forms another *inclusio* much like the two designated signs that took place in Cana and enclosed the stories in what I have called the Cana Cycle. While the first cycle focused on believing, the focus in this cycle has been on conflict between Jesus and the Jews, particularly the leadership, which is the basic reason the evangelist in writing the prologue says that Jesus came to his own (historic) place (*idia*) and his own (historic) people (*idioi*) did not receive him (1:11).

The signs that Jesus had done in the second cycle—from the healing of a miserable paralytic, through the feeding of an immense crowd with a donated lunch of five loaves and two fish, to his strange phenomenon of walking on the sea, and then to the amazing healing of a man born blind—should have convinced fair-minded people that a unique messenger from God had been in their midst. But the commitment of the Jews to their ideological and theological presuppositions only made them more convinced concerning the blasphemous claim of Jesus that he and the Father were "one." Remaining issues still must be determined: Could the power of Jesus extend beyond the grave to the locked chambers of *Sheol*? And would such power change their minds?[80] Those questions are faced in this climactic story to which we now turn.

This story opens with Jesus in the north of the country when a desperate message is sent from the south to him from Martha and Mary (or perhaps another Mary, but—not likely Magdalene, as some suggest) concerning Lazarus, Jesus' friend in Bethany near Jerusalem (11:1-3).[81] But then the evangelist tells us Jesus responds that "the illness would not end in death."

---

80 See my discussion of "Excursus 10: Signs and Presuppositions" in G. Borchert, *John 1–11*, 346–48.

81 There is an interesting variant at this point in P 66 that changed the text from "the village of Mary and of Mary his sister" to "Mary and Martha her sister," which has led to some scholars speculating with Elizabeth Schrader that this second Mary may be "Magdalene." That suggestion is rather unlikely, however, since "Magdalene" is generally attached to her name. See also the note on the anointing (below).

Instead, it would turn out "for the glory of God—and the Son of God would be glorified through it" (11:4). Those words have a strangely familiar ring to them: they remind us of the deeply emotional prayer of Jesus when he later would pray that the glory of the Son might glorify God (17:1).

Yet, immediately after this powerful insight into the self-effacing Jesus, there seems to be a fuzzy double statement—both that Jesus loves the family of Lazarus and that Jesus stays two extra days in that same place. (Translators here have had a notoriously difficult time bringing together the love of friends and the travel delay.[82] What shall we conclude? Surely God and Jesus love humans and care about human suffering.)

[I urge you not to build any theological theories about God and suffering on the few such textual phenomena in your Bible. Of course, it would be resolved. But phenomenal time issues often trouble us humans because we treat time as a constant reality. But our storyteller had learned to think and write beyond time and space constancies.]

When the evangelist continues the story, Jesus next tells the disciples that he is returning to Judea. That announcement is hardly to their liking because they remind Jesus that the Jews there are ready to stone him (11:8). Jesus responds with a mini sermon: He understands timing and the difference between walking in day and in the night. Moreover, he reminds them about "the light of the world" (11:9). Then he tells them that Lazarus is asleep and that he will awaken him. The disciples, who want no more encounters in Judea, quickly reply that Lazarus could easily recover from sleep. But Jesus informs them that "Lazarus is dead!" and then adds: "I am glad that I was not there so that you might believe." Do the disciples understand what Jesus is suggesting?

Their realist, Thomas—who is hardly a stick figure in this story—paints a dismal picture when he says to the rest of the disciples, "Let's go ... and die with him" (11:16). Is Thomas fearful? Probably. Is he a coward? Not likely. His response is one of resignation at the prospect of trouble and possible death. But if Jesus is going south, to the south the disciples will also go!

---

82 Our NLT translators inserted an extra "although" in v. 5 to make the sentences hang together. However one may translate these verses, there is no warrant for thinking that Jesus was being hardhearted with the family of Lazarus.

When they arrive in Judea, they discover that Lazarus has indeed been dead for four days[83] and the funeral proceedings will soon be concluding. Then Martha goes to meet Jesus and says to him, "Lord, if only you had been here, my brother would not have died" (11:21). She also adds, "But even now I know that God will give you what you ask." These words come from one who has grieved deeply and realizes that the inevitable has come to pass.

As the story continues, Jesus replies, "Your brother will rise again." Martha responds that she has been taught well and knows resurrection theology. Like most of the working population who has been influenced by Pharisaic teachers, she knows that her brother will rise at the end of time. Then it is as though Jesus raises his hand and declares to Martha: "I am the resurrection and the life.[84] Anyone who believes in me, even if that person dies, will live!" Moreover, Jesus continues: "Everyone who lives and believes in me will never die." Then looking directly at her, he asks Martha: "Do you believe what I am saying?" Martha's answer is a classic confession: "Yes, Lord, I believe you are the Christ, the Son of God, the [promised] one who is coming into the world" (11:27).

The dialogue ends at that point. It may seem complete, but these words are not the end of the conversation. So, I warn you: Be very careful with these words, or you may misunderstand the story!

Martha leaves the scene and calls her sister, Mary, who follows her to meet Jesus.[85] When the mourners see Mary leave the house, they follow, thinking she is going to the tomb. Instead, she meets Jesus and falls at his feet crying: "Lord if only you had been here, my bother would not have died" (11:32).

---

83 The statement "four days" was very important to the evangelist and to Jewish thinking about death, because after three days the spirit of the person was presumed to have left the vicinity of the body. See, e.g., James P. Martin, "History and Eschatology in the Lazarus Narrative, John 11:1–44," *Scottish Journal of Theology* 17 (1964), 332–43 and R. Dunkerly, "Lazarus," *NTS* 5 (1955), 321–27.

84 Some scholars such as Bultmann (*Gospel of John*, 492–03) and Schnackenburg (St. John, 2. 331–32) have argued that this assertion of Jesus that he is both "resurrection and life" is unnecessary redundancy. But the statement reflects the evangelist's double-level thinking concerning the two realms of reality that I have discussed frequently in my commentary. See G. Borchert, *John 1–11*, 356.

85 Several scholars have sought to identify different characteristics in Mary and Martha in the stories of Luke 10:38-42 and John 11:1-38 and 12:2-3. For an example of this approach, see T. Pollard, "The Raising of Lazarus," *Studia Evangelia* 6 (1973), 434–43.

When Jesus sees her and the mourners in deep anguish wailing,[86] he is greatly troubled (angered) in his spirit, and he asks where Lazarus is buried. When they take him to the tomb, Jesus weeps (11:15).

I have often asked myself why Jesus wept. Why did the Christian scribes make these words the shortest verse in the Bible? Why did the evangelist tell us that some mourners were asking "Could he who opened the eyes of the blind not have kept Lazarus from dying?" Of course, Jesus loved Lazarus. But why was Jesus so troubled? He already knew that he was going to raise Lazarus. He even told his disciples that he would do so—before he left the north for the south. The answer may be that he encountered something in the south that he had not quite expected, something that troubled his spirit greatly. What was it?

I am convinced that the answer lies in the people who could confess their belief in Jesus but who could not conceive of him being God in the flesh and having power over death. I am convinced of this answer because of what happened when Jesus approached the tomb and told the people to remove the stone. Just then, Martha, the great confessor, spoke: "Lord, he has been in the tomb four days, and by this time, he stinks!" (11:39).

[Consider Martha's statements: "Lord, I believe" and "Lord ... he stinks." In those two statements lies a vivid commentary on human frailty and misunderstanding: Our words do not necessarily represent reality. Allow me to illustrate: Some years ago, an eminent New Testament scholar and friend from the European continent who had written several commentaries was preaching from this text at a seminary in America and focused on Martha and her confession. He was instructive about believing and confessing, but he failed to mention Martha's statement at the tomb. When I questioned him on his failure, he admitted the weakness of his sermon. I use this illustration as a reminder that we never get beyond the point that we can learn, but primarily because this story is so crucial to understanding how frail and imperfect may be our confessions about Jesus. Please take this warning seriously. Death is the one physical enemy that humans cannot handle well without God. We may confess our belief in God and in Jesus, as Martha did, but death is the ultimate test for humanity concerning what we believe. The old man we call John who was the source behind this magnificent gospel understood that facing death squarely is the ultimate test for believing.]

---

86 I would agree with George Beasley-Murray that English translators often render the wailing, which angered Jesus, so politely that the emotions of the story are underplayed. See Beasley-Murray, *John*, 192–93.

In answer to Martha's pleas about the body stinking, Jesus responds by telling her that if she would believe, she "would see the glory of God" (11:40). Then without further delay or distraction Jesus prays, "Father, thank you for hearing me."[87] Then he shouts to the body in the tomb, "Lazarus, come out!" That is all it took! Out of the tomb emerges the man—tied in his grave wrappings. Then Jesus directs the mourners to "Untie him, and let him go." (What do you think they wanted to do when they saw that body coming out of the tomb?)

The Lazarus story is like few others, and no doubt has been retold many times. While some observers/hearers become believers, others rush quickly to inform the Pharisees and members of the Sanhedrin of these shocking events. The council is quickly called into session, because such an event would not go unnoticed in the politics of the day. The Romans are sure to get wind of this incredible miracle worker. But in the turmoil of the council (the Great Sanhedrin), Caiaphas (the high priest), after scolding the members for their ignorance concerning politics, issues his well-known dictum that "It is expedient for you that one man should die for the people than that the whole nation should be destroyed." The Johannine evangelist finds this dictum to be prophetic. In fact, it is a prediction of the ultimate impact that the unique death of Jesus would have upon the children of God throughout the world (11:51-52).

The council must make an ultimate decision—a fatal decision. Jesus would have to die! So, the council begins to plot his death. Jesus clearly understands the impact of that decision: most of his public ministry would come to a screeching halt. Accordingly, he withdraws to the wilderness near Ephraim. To emphasize that the end is now on the horizon, the evangelist issues his announcement that the Passover is near. That haunting refrain will echo and re-echo throughout the second half of the gospel. The Festival Cycle is now finished, and the first half of the Johannine gospel has come to an end.

Still, Jesus has not yet been arrested, although the order for his arrest has been issued. Neither he nor his disciples have been imprisoned, although such is now a clear possibility. But the questions begin to swirl concerning this unique person we call Jesus: Will he attend the Passover? If so, how will he come? What will his coming mean for the disciples? Indeed, what will it mean for the world? These questions are the focus of the second half of these fascinating stories we call the Gospel of John.

---

87 I would remind you that the evangelist signals when Jesus is praying because he addresses God directly as "Father" (*pater*). See 11:41b-42, 12:27-28, 17:1-26.

Part 2

The Bible's Transforming Storybook

Hour, Farewell, Death, and Resurrection

Chapter 4

Jesus' Entry into Jerusalem and the Arrival of the Haunting Hour (12:1-50)

With perhaps only the prologue, chapter 12 of John is one of the most tightly knit and compact sections in the gospel. This chapter functions as a major saddle between two mountain peaks, and here it links the two major sections of this highly organized gospel. All the persons in this fascinating chapter function more like stick figures rather than as round characters, except for the King and Savior, Jesus—the only character who is highlighted throughout the chapter. The purpose naturally is to focus on him and to define his role as clearly as possible. Pondering the segments of this chapter then should help the reader to arrive at a better understanding of who the evangelist envisions Jesus to be and what he considers to be the purpose or goal of his wonderful stories.

The chapter also serves as a forceful introduction to the second half of the gospel and can easily be divided into five brief sections that can help the reader sense the various strains of the storyteller's thinking. These small segments are the anointing (12:1-8), the linking transition (12:9-11), the pre-Passover entry into Jerusalem and the various views about Jesus (12:12-22), the perspective of Jesus and the critical turning point in the story (12:23-36), the summarizing implications and the significance of believing (12:37-50).[88]

The Anointing (12:1-8)

The fact that there is an anointing story in all four canonical gospels confirms that for the early church the anointing was viewed as a strategic event in the proclamation of the gospel. Yet if one simply consults the church's earliest

---

88   See my earlier analysis of this chapter in G. Borchert, *John 12–21*, 31–70.

harmony of the Gospels (the *Diatessaron of Tatian* from the second century),[89] one will quickly discover that there are considerable differences in the gospel presentations of the event. These differences involve several questions:

- On what part of Jesus' body did the anointing take place: his head (Mark/Matthew) or his feet (Luke/John)?
- Where did the anointing take place: in the home of Simon the leper (Mark/Matthew), or the home of Simon the Pharisee (Luke), or in Bethany at the home of Mary, Martha (?), and Lazarus (John 11:1-2)?
- When did the anointing take place: after a meeting with Jewish leaders two days before Passover (Mark /Matthew), or six days before Passover (John), or not sure (Luke)?
- Who performed the anointing: a sinful woman (Luke), an unidentified woman (Mark/Matthew), or Mary of Bethany (probably John)—which has led some commentators to identify her with Mary Magdalene (a construct by readers from Luke and John)?

As a result of such confusions, some scholars, including A.T. Robertson, have posited two anointings[90] much like some have suggested there are two cleansings of the Temple. But there is only one cleansing and one anointing in each gospel.[91]

   While it is not impossible that there were two anointings (perhaps one in Galilee and one south in Judea), we should have learned from the story of the cleansing of the Temple that the Johannine evangelist is not tied to our twenty-first-century Western understanding of chronological order: the storyteller is more interested in readers getting the point of his organizational order. In this case, the anointing story forms the introduction to the death story of Jesus and clearly impacts the second part of the gospel. The anointing must come before

---

89 See, e.g., H. Hill, *The Earliest Life of Christ Ever Compiled from the Four Gospels Being the Diatessaron of Tatian* (Edinburgh: T&T Clark, 1804) and A.S. Marmarji, Diatessaron De Tatien (Beymouth: Impremerie Catholique, 1935).

90 See A.T. Robertson, *A Harmony of the Gospels* (New York: Harper, 1922), 60. The identification of this Mary of Bethany with Mary Magdalene has been given new life because of some recent research by Elizabeth Schrader concerning a confusion of words at 11:1 in Codex P 66, but that issue remains quite tentative and is unresolved.

91 See G. Borchert, *John 12–21*, 33, esp. at fn. 9.

the entry to provide the Johannine perspective on that entry. The decision that Jesus must die has already been made by the dictum of Caiaphas, which concludes part 1 of the gospel.

In the Synoptic Gospels the anointing hardly plays such a strategic role. The two crucial events in the organization of the other gospels are the powerful entry into Jerusalem, followed by the forceful cleansing of the Temple that set the stage for the condemnation of Jesus by the Jews. This distinction is crucial for understanding John. (The storyteller is a very astute Christian writer and editor, not a pedantic newspaper reporter!)

Remember that many of these stories likely circulated as individual oral pericopes about Jesus before they were combined and edited into complete works. Their individuality can be recognized by some lingering elements from their past.[92] The complete Lazarus story provides an excellent example of this fact for John because Mary is introduced a chapter earlier (11:2) as the one "who anointed the Lord with ointment and wiped his feet with her hair." That story was undoubtedly known in the Johannine community before it would have been read in a written form.

But the reader should quickly realize the nature of chapter 12. Here Mary and Martha are more like one-dimensional stick figures serving as single-purpose characters than they are in chapter 11. Mary's role is as burial anointer,[93] and Martha's role is that of a food preparer so the event can take place.[94] The role of Judas Iscariot is that of villain who has no redeemable qualities and is nothing but a thief. He is present to provide Jesus with the foil for announcing his forthcoming death and burial and for contradicting any suggestion that Jesus might be self-serving in accepting what might be interpreted as a royal burial with no interest in the poor (12:8). Yet I have no doubt that the early Christians viewed the value of the anointing as a symbolic indication that a king was being anointed for burial (cf. 19:39-41).

---

92 See G. Borchert, *John 12–21*, 34.

93 It is intriguing to note that the word used for the amount of spice is reckoned in terms of *litra* (usually translated as "pound"). It is found in the New Testament only here at 12:3 and at 19:39.

94 The figure of Mary here is quite different than the woman in Luke 7:44-48. There is no mention of sinfulness or remorse here. The entire focus of the stories is different. The story in Mark (14:9) and Matthew (26:13) is similar in that it is a proclamation, but the anointing is of the head and not the feet.

The Linking Transition
(12:9-11)

The storyteller concludes Part 1 with the decision that Jesus must "die for the people" (11:50). Part 2 begins with the anointing scene (12:3) and then links the two parts of his magnificent gospel story by reintroducing the crowd— which is a major concern of the council. The crowd, having learned that Jesus is in Bethany, seeks to find both him and Lazarus—which means that the high priests are forced to consider eliminating the two of them (12:10). The people now have exhibit number one of why they should believe in the immense power and authority of Jesus (12:11). Time is obviously at hand for the authorities to arrange for the arrest of Jesus.

The Pre-Passover Entry into Jerusalem and the
Various Views about Jesus
(12:12-22)

Then what the council greatly fears, in fact, does take place. The huge Passover crowd hears that Jesus is coming to Jerusalem. They go out to welcome him, carrying palm branches and chanting their messianic acclamations: "Hosanna! Blessed is he who comes in the name of the Lord! Indeed, the King of Israel!" (12:13; cf. Ps 118:25, 26). Then as Jesus acquires a young donkey and rides it, the evangelist quotes a messianic text to elucidate this exciting experience: "Don't be afraid, daughter of Zion; behold your king is coming, sitting on a donkey's colt" (12:15; cf. Zech 9:9).

It seems like party time for the people who have been under the domination of Rome and longing for freedom and release from their captive status. But what does all this excitement mean, especially for Jesus who earlier seemed to eschew popularity and who retreated into the hills when they tried to make him King after he fed the multitude (6:15)? I believe that the evangelist is prepared to evaluate the various perspectives. The crowd is ready to make Jesus their king.

But what about the disciples? Their reaction seems to be one of confusion. The ways of Jesus are not easy for them to understand, but the evangelist informs us that after Jesus was "glorified," the disciples were able to piece things together—including the Lazarus events—so that it later makes sense (12:16-18).

The Pharisees, on the other hand, are completely frustrated. Their plans to remove Jesus from the scene (and Lazarus if necessary) and pretend that everything can return to the status quo seems to implode—as if a Jesus revolution is happening before their eyes (12:19).

Then the storyteller adds another group: the Greeks. (I have often wondered: Did the evangelist mean Hellenistic Jews who had come for Passover, or was he being more expansive in his thinking since he was writing this gospel from Asia Minor many years later?) The Hellenists approach Phillip (who will later minister in Asia Minor),[95] apparently seeking an opportunity to join the exciting events. Philip in turn locates Andrew, one of the disciples from the early inner circle, and they both approach Jesus about these Greeks (12:20-22).[96]

The Perspective of Jesus and the Critical Turning Point in the Story (12:23-33)

But then something strange happens. It is almost as though the bell tolls and the excitement stops. Then Jesus announces: "The hour has come for the Son of Man to be glorified" (12:23). There is no question about the change. All the other perspectives about the events related to the entry into Jerusalem seem to explode in a puff of smoke as Jesus issues another of his double *amēn* oath-like sayings: "Unless a grain of wheat falls into the earth and dies, it continues by itself; but if it dies it produces an abundant crop" (12:24). Indeed, Jesus continues by stating that the one "who hates his life in this world will keep it for eternal life" (12:25).[97]

It is as though the idea of a so-called "triumphal entry" into Jerusalem has been given an entirely new meaning. It is here viewed as an entry into

---

95 The Martyrion (Memorial) to the Apostle Philip and tomb was discovered in recent years at Hierapolis. See G. Borchert, *Lands of the Bible: In the Footsteps of Paul and John*, vol. 2 (Cleveland, TN: Mossy Creek Press, 2012), 85–87.

96 For Don Carson's attempt at harmonizing the gospel stories here, see Carson, *John*, 436. See also Beasley-Murray, *John*, 211. For Robert Fortna's approach at reconstruction, see *The Fourth Gospel and Its Predecessor* (Philadelphia: Fortress, 1988), 120–48. See my comments in G. Borchert, *John 12–21*, 47.

97 Readers are reminded of the Semitic frequent use of absolutistic contrasts such as love and hate: for example, Jacob's love for Rachel and hate for Leah (Gen 29:30-31) or the Lord loving Jacob and hating Esau (Mal 1:2, Rom 9:13). Cf. also the old theory of loving one's neighbor and hating the enemy (Matt 5:43).

death, an entry into sacrifice, an entry into self-giving, an entry into "eternal life" with Jesus (12:25). Indeed, the Johannine storyteller sees the entry into Jerusalem as an invitation to serve and to follow Jesus (12:26). But the entry is not easy for Jesus. Rather, it is excruciating. It is an emptying experience that leads him to an agonizing prayer that he might "be saved" from this "hour." Yet he knows that he cannot retreat from his destined purpose. So, he begs that the "Father" would be glorified through his entry to Jerusalem.

At this special time, as Jesus wrestles with his defining death, the Johannine evangelist employs "the voice from heaven" to confirm Jesus' transformative decision to accept his destiny and "glorify" God (12:28).[98] The people hardly understand the eternal significance of this event. To some, the voice sounds like a crack of thunder; others think an angel has addressed Jesus (12:29). Jesus then tells them that the voice is provided not for his benefit but for theirs, and that an eschatological turning point in history has arrived, which is none other than the judgment of the world—namely, the defeat of evil and its controlling authority through the "lifting up" or crucifying of Jesus (cf.3:14). This strategic act is the means God will use to draw humans to himself (12:32).

The crowd now understands that Jesus will die, and they challenge his view of the Messiah because they are sure that the "Christ" and his messianic kingdom will last forever (12:34). Jesus is not about to enter another theological debate, however, and he simply tells them that the light is still present in their midst and their responsibility is to walk while they still have light and to believe in him. Then Jesus departs and simply hides from them (12:35-36).

The Summarizing Implications and the Significance of Believing (12:37-50)

When we pick up the story again, the Johannine evangelist returns to the theme of the people not believing, even though Jesus has done many signs among them. But as an interpreter of the Jesus story, the storyteller understands that this refusal on the part of the people fulfills multiple predictions found in texts such as Isaiah 6, 9, 10, and 53. On the other hand, he knows

---

98   Here is the only use of the heavenly voice in the Gospel of John. In the Synoptic Gospels the voice is mentioned in connection with the baptism of Jesus and the transfiguration. In Mark 1:11 and Luke 3:22 the voice confirms that Jesus pleases God, whereas in Matt 3:17 the voice is used to announce who Jesus is. In the transfiguration stories the voice corrects the disciples' misunderstanding of who Jesus is (cf. Mark 9:5-7, Matt 17:4-6, Luke 9:33-35).

there are many who believe in Jesus, even among the Jewish authorities. But they refuse to confess him because of their fear of being excommunicated from the synagogue and because they prefer human praise to divine acceptance (12:37-43).

Then in a magnificent conclusion (12:44-50) to this introduction to the Death Story, the evangelist pictures Jesus as an ancient prophet crying out in desperation to a shocked audience—perhaps from a dark, empty stage:

"Believing in me means believing in God who sent me."
"Seeing me means seeing God."
"I came as Light so you don't have to walk in darkness."
"I did not come to judge but to save the world."
"Don't treat my words casually…you will regret doing so."
"My words will be your judge on the last day."
"I am not speaking on my own authority, but by the authority of the Father."
"Remember: his message brings eternal life. Listen to him."

What a way to finish this beginning to the second half of John's gospel. Every time I read this text, shivers creep up my back in an overwhelming reaction and I want to cry out: "Listen to Jesus, friends! Listen to Jesus!"

Chapter 5

Stories of Preparation and the Farewell Cycle
(13:1–17:26)

With the closing words of John 12 ringing in our ears, I turn to the Farewell Cycle, which provides the evangelist with both the model of Jesus and a summary of the Lord's farewell instructions for his followers. As I have indicated in my larger commentary,[99] it is helpful to visualize chapters 13–17 in the form of a bullseye/target having a center and three rings (or a chiastic ["X"] form with outside layers and a crossing point):

The outer ring (or segments) focus(es) on the two actions of Jesus: his washing of the disciples' feet and the giving of a new commandment (13:1-38) and his magnificent prayer (17:1-26). The penultimate ring (or segments) is/are composed of issues of loneliness and anxiety (14:1-14, 16:16-33). The inner ring (or segments) deal(s) with the five Paraclete or Holy Spirit passages (14:15-31, 15:26–16:15). The center of the bullseye (or crossing point of the chiasm) involves the second great *mashal* of John (15:1-25).

It is important to have one of these balanced picture models in mind as we discuss the individual texts, as it should help us perceive just how brilliant is this artistic storyteller.[100]

Judas, Peter, and Perceiving Foot Washing as a Key to Discipleship
(13:1-38)

The evangelist opens the Farewell Cycle by quickly providing the details necessary for engaging the story. The haunting "hour" has arrived, so the crucial Passover is just around the corner. The love of Jesus for his followers, and his commitment to them, is clearly undiminished. He is fully in charge

---

99 For a diagram, see G. Borchert, *John 12–21*, 74–76.

100 As we approach these chapters, it is important to know that many scholars have difficulty treating them as coming from one unified source. Indeed, they find seams throughout these chapters and argue for different theological perspectives evident in them. For example, Schnackenburg (*St. John*, 3. 23) thinks that in 13:12-20 the death of Jesus is not in focus. I strongly disagree with his perspective.

of the setting and since he knows God's will, he is completely aware of the traitorous actions of the devil-man, Judas (13:1-3).

The group is ready for dinner,[101] but then Jesus does the unexpected: He rises, takes off his outer garments, wraps a towel around himself, pours water into a bowl, and to the shock of the disciples starts to wash their feet. He is making good progress in this service until he comes to Peter—the dear disciple who sometimes thinks he understands Jesus but often misses the point. When Peter sees his Lord demeaning himself as a common servant, he attempts to correct Jesus. But even when Jesus informs him that he will understand later, Peter asserts his unwillingness to have Jesus wash his feet (13:8). When Jesus explains that refusal would mean that Peter is not part of Jesus, Peter then humorously asks Jesus for a full shower. But this episode is no humorous matter: that ring of disciples includes one who is not part of Jesus—he is a betrayer (13:11).

Then Jesus finally gives the disciples an interpretation of his actions: As their "Teacher" and "Lord," he has washed their feet: likewise, they should wash one another's feet (13:12-14). And he forcefully reminds his disciples in a double *amēn* oath-like saying that "a servant is not greater than his master." They would be blessed, he adds, if they could understand the reality of their task as servants.

[I must pause here and note that after studying and writing for many years, I remain surprised that foot washing never actually became a sacrament or ordinance of the church—especially since it is related to an express command of Jesus. Yet I suspect that it has been spiritualized to such an extent that many Christians consider they are fulfilling the Lord's command. I wonder, however, if our concepts of servanthood have also been so spiritualized that we use the words but lack the spirit of servants. I cannot help but remember that between the Eastern and the Western bishops of Constantinople and Rome, there developed a fierce contest concerning who was primary. The East chose "Ecumenical Patriarch," and the West chose the "Servant of the Servants of

---

101 Scholarship is highly divided on whether this meal is a Passover meal and whether it is also the Lord's Supper (a designation that does not appear in the Gospel of John; cf.1 Cor 11:20). Marcus Barth (*Das Abendmahl: Passamahl, Bundesmahl und Messiasmahl* ThST 18 [1945]) links all three together. J. Jeremias (*The Eucharistic Words of Jesus* [New York: Scribner, 1966]) views the Lord's Supper and the Passover meal as one. E. Gaugler (*Das Abendmahl in Neuen Testament* [1943]) is not quite sure the Passover meal and the Supper are the same. For a review of this issue, see B. Klappert, "The Lord's Supper," *Dictionary of New Testament Theology,* 2.520–38. See G. Borchert, *John 12–21,* 76–78.

God." Is vying for honor what servanthood means for us? This question is a searching one for all Christians.]

Jesus again identifies himself with the "I am" (*egō eimi*) of Israel's historic God (13:19; cf. Exod 3:14) and turns the disciples' attention to their future task as his agents of mission. Prefacing his message with another double *amēn* oath-like statement, he indicates that those who would receive the disciples and their witness in the future would actually be receiving him and the Father who sent him (13:20).

Jesus has unloaded an exceedingly complex message on the bewildered disciples. Are they ready for it? (I have some genuine doubts!) One thing is clear: Jesus is troubled. So, in another double *amēn* statement, he makes his concern evident: One of his disciples will betray him. The troubling issue has been set before his disciples, resulting in even greater bewilderment among the group. The disciples probably then start to eye each other suspiciously. A villain is in their room—a devil man! But they will soon learn that behind him there is a greater villain: the figure of Satan.[102]

Peter, however, will not wait for further clarity. He wants the inside scoop immediately. So, he signals his desire for more information to the beloved disciple[103] who is lying next to the breast (*en tō kolpō*)[104] of Jesus, as they are all stretched out for the meal around the triclinium table (13:23-24).[105] Tenseness surely abounds: it certainly is not a period for hiding the truth. So, Jesus responds by identifying the traitor as the one to whom he will give a dipped

---

102 C.S. Lewis portrayed the incidents in the biblical story in a priceless way with his story of Aslan and the White Witch in *The Lion, the Witch, and the Wardrobe* (New York: Macmillan, 1950).

103 The use of the term "the beloved disciple" or "the one whom Jesus loved" (*agapa ho iesous*) is first identified here in the Farewell Cycle. See 13:23; cf. 19:26; 20:2; 21;7, 20. See also M. Morton, "The Beloved Disciple Again," *StudBib II* (Sheffield: Sheffield, 1980), 216–18.

104 The reference to the Beloved Disciple lying on the breast of Jesus (13:23) should remind the reader of the similar expression of Jesus being in the breast (*eis ton kolpon*) of the Father in the prologue of John (1:18).

105 A triclinium arrangement was a low, wide, U-shaped table around which the guests would be gathered. The legs of those eating would normally be stretched behind them, and they would prop themselves up on one elbow and use the other arm and hand to lift the food to the mouth after having dipped it into the sauces supplied. The master of the feast would often, but not always, be positioned in the center or cross part of the "U."

piece of food.[106] (Just think of where Judas may have been reclining when Jesus handed him the morsel of food. Could he have been as close as at the back of Jesus?[107] What a picture that would be!)

Jesus gives the morsel of food to Judas, and he eats it. Then, as if the clock strikes the "bewitching hour," Satan enters Judas. Jesus directs Judas to do his deed of betrayal—and quickly. Then Jesus dismisses him from the group!

Although some of the disciples are not sure what Jesus' instructions to Judas mean, the storyteller informs us that when Judas leaves the scene, the curtain of "night" drops (13:30). It must have been a chilling moment—a time when everything seemed to go dark.

When we next pick up the story, Jesus announces: "Now is the Son of Man glorified!" As we read this gospel—even today—talk about "glory" hardly has a dark side to it. We are customarily not thinking about death and dying, but the death story of Jesus has redefined the meaning of glorification and the understanding of "glory" for Christians (13:31-32). When Jesus tries to explain to the disciples what this event means, he reminds them as he told the Jews, "Where I am going, you cannot come" (13:33; cf. 7:34). The picture is clear in the mind of Jesus: He is focused on his coming death, but it is hardly on the minds of the disciples.

Also, during these tense moments Jesus issues what has become known as the defining new commandment for his followers: "Love one another, even as I have loved you" (13:34). This command is among the simplest statements in the Bible, yet it is among the most profound messages ever delivered to humanity. Love is the intended characteristic of every follower of Jesus, but it remains among the most underachieved goals of Christians. The command to love one another has never been withdrawn and continues to challenge every follower of Jesus. Indeed, Jesus highlights the significance of such love as the crucial key for everyone knowing "that you are my disciples" (13:35).

(Sadly, it seems easier to talk about loving one another than to do so. Words such as "love" unfortunately can easily drip off our tongues without

---

106 Scholars have various views on the meaning of the morsel that Jesus handed to Judas, views ranging from a magical act to the termination of a relationship with Jesus. Beasley-Murray, citing a suggestion from Leslie Newbigin, posited an interesting thought that the act of Jesus in giving Judas the morsel was an act of love that made Judas decide whether he would follow through on betraying Jesus. See Beasley-Murray, *John*, 238–39. Cf. also Carson, *John*, 474–75. For other suggestions, see G. Borchert, *John 12–21*, 94.

107 For a detailed explanation of my speculations on this possibility, see G. Borchert, *John 12–21*, 92, esp. in fn. 59.

having any attachment to our lives and actions. So, they readily can render the Christian witness to be a phantom shadow of reality. But to "love one another, even as I have loved you" is the Christian's equivalent of the British *Magna Carta*. It is the foundation of Christian existence.)

With the command of Jesus to love one another, one would be tempted to conclude the foot-washing story, but the evangelist has one more video clip to complete before he finishes his introduction to the Farewell Cycle. For the third time in this brief episode, Peter comes front and center in the story. Again, he speaks without understanding the scope of his words. When he hears Jesus say that the disciples will not be able to follow Jesus now, he challenges Jesus. Instead of understanding what Jesus has said, Peter proclaims that he will lay down his life for Jesus. (The Lord must have shaken his head and replied, "Will you...?") Then, issuing another double *amēn* saying, Jesus concludes with the incisive words: "Before the rooster crows, you will deny me three times" (13:38).

Understanding Loneliness and Anxiety among the Disciples[108]
(14:1-14)

The Johannine evangelist was a spellbinding storyteller. He really knew how to leave his readers waiting for the next episode. The chill that enveloped the previous scene when Judas was dismissed from the dinner has now settled over the disciples, and the reality of evil that could be ahead is seizing them. Naturally they are filled with questions and worries. Jesus had talked about going somewhere they could not come. Where is he going? They are filled with anxiety. Is Jesus going to leave them and abandon them to the Jewish administrative wolves? They quickly begin to realize that Jesus has been their security net. What will happen to them if he is gone? The feeling of loneliness begins to mushroom in the minds of the disciples. It is very unsettling. Would Jesus understand the emptiness of their feelings?

Then Jesus tells the disciples that he knows they are worried and anxious, but not to be troubled and instead to trust him because believing in God is like believing in him (14:1). Then he shifts his focus and starts talking about going to prepare a place for them and that his Father's estate/domain (*oikia*) has

---

108 In contrast to many scholars who think this section involves 13:31–14:31, I believe there is a division at 14:14. See, e.g., F. Segovia, "The Structure and Sitz-im-Leben of John 13:31–14:31," *JBL* 104 (1985): 471–93 and Beasley-Murray, *John*, 243.

many "resting places" (*monai*)—not "mansions"[109]—for them. It is as though Jesus is going someplace and that it involves their future, but his words do not compute for the disciples.

(I do believe that the early readers of John, unlike those disciples in the story, did have a sense that Jesus was speaking eschatologically, but I wonder if we sometimes have difficulty realizing what the storyteller meant. I am pretty sure, however, that his listeners/readers would understand the dialogue of Jesus. I think that this text clearly implies a futuristic perspective. Some scholars, however, have been influenced by C.H. Dodd's realized eschatology and the theories of R. Bultmann who argued that such views should be attributed to Gnostic or pre-Mandean mythologies that dismiss the futurism here.[110] I think we frequently create contexts for such speeches that would be unrecognizable to the early readers.)

As Jesus is making these statements, Thomas speaks up and interjects his concerns. Thomas is the realist among the disciples and the one who had earlier recognized the potential of their death in the south when Lazarus had died (11:16). While Jesus is trying to explain to the group about their being with him and that they know where he is going, Thomas stops Jesus and tells him that the disciples do not have a clue about where he is headed or the way to get there (14:5). He interprets Jesus as going on a journey and, therefore, he wants the specifics related to that travel. Jesus responds: "I am the way, the truth and the life" and no one gets to the Father except by him (14:6).

(In discussing verse 6, Bultmann focuses on "the way as a pure expression of revelation" over against content that reminds us of his dynamic writings on "faith" and his pattern of playing down "truth and life" much the way his writings do so on "knowledge," leaving readers wondering about the content of believing and reminiscent of his division between the Jesus of history and the Christ of faith.)[111]

---

109 The Greek word *monai* (from the verb *menein*) was rendered into the Latin as *mansio*, which was translated unfortunately in the Tyndale version and then in the KJV as "mansions." The word is not advocating a prosperity gospel. See B. Newman and E. Nida, *A Translator's Handbook of the Gospel of John* (London: United Bible Societies, 1980), 454.

110 See, e.g., C.H. Dodd, *The Interpretation of the Fourth Gospel* (Cambridge: University Press, 1958), 404 and Bultmann, *John*, 602.

111 See Bultmann, *John*, 605. For my further discussion on this subject, see G. Borchert, *John 12–21*, 109–10. Also see the difference in the way Bultmann treats "faith" and "knowledge" in *TDNT* 6.1 74–82, 197–228 and 1. 689–719.

To continue the frustration of the disciples, we note that all the talk about the "Father" is just too much for Philip. Finally. in exasperation he says to Jesus, "Just show us the Father and we can get on with our anxiety" (14:8). Jesus catches Philip in his frustration, and probably responds with something akin to: "Oh Philip! Don't you know by now that 'the one who has seen me has seen the Father.' How can you ask to see the Father?" (14:9-10). (If I were writing this message, I might have added: "Philip, do you want to be dead?")

As I have reflected many times on this story, I come away realizing again and again how difficult it must have been for those early disciples to understand Jesus and what he was saying to them. It is one thing for us to read this story many years later and know that in the resurrection Jesus conquered death; it was quite another matter for the early disciples to face this man Jesus who looked very human and who needed food and sleep, and then hear him say "Believe that I am in the Father and the Father is in me"—or at least believe because of the works you see me doing (14:11).

Believing is not easy, especially when the evangelist uses another double *amēn* oath-like statement to assert that "the one who believes in me will do the works I do, and even greater works, because I am going to the Father" (14:12). This pericope then ends by assuring us, the readers, that glory will be given to God when we "ask anything in my name and I will do it" (14:13-14; 15:7, 16).[112] I wonder how you react to those words. Do you take them seriously? What do they mean? Of course, they do not mean that God is like a spineless Santa Claus and is ready to give us anything we want. Remember: God did not seem ready to grant Jesus a positive answer when he prayed for the cup of suffering to be removed (Luke 22:42; cf. John 12:27-28).

Certainly, praying or asking God for something cannot mean if we simply append "in the name of Jesus" to our prayer that we will get what we ask. To pray in the name of Jesus (15:16) means to pray in the nature or spirit of Jesus. When Jesus prayed, he quickly realized that to pray for the cup of suffering to be removed was not the will of God, so he soon reversed his prayer (Luke 22:42). To believe and to pray believing is nothing less than to become like Jesus. Accordingly, for the Johannine storyteller, believing prayer is not simply an intellectual affirmation. Believing prayer involves a trusting commitment of the whole self to Jesus—the Lamb of God who takes away the sin of the

---

112 For my further discussion of "The Significance of Prayer for the Christian," see G. Borchert, *Tension*, 134–42.

world (John 1:29). That kind of believing prayer is what brings glory to God and is foundational to understanding the Johannine view of the Holy Spirit in the lives of believers.

Introducing the First Two Paraclete/Holy Spirit Passages (14:15-31)

We come now to the first major section of the Paraclete or Spirit passages in John. The evangelist must have pondered these texts for some time because of his insights and the way the ideas all fit together. The first Paraclete passage begins with a fascinating condition: "If you love me, keep my commandments and I will ask the Father and he will give you another Counselor (*parakleton*) to be with you forever" (14:15-16). This text likely means that the Counselor would serve as an alter ego for Jesus.[113] The focus here is on love and obedience.

You will remember that love is the subject of the new commandment, with a focus on loving one another (13:34). Here the focus of love shifts just slightly to loving Jesus, which is the foundation for understanding and relating to God. But the love here is not that of individually-minded people.[114] The verb *agapate* is in the plural—like most of the verbs in this section—and thus implies a community living in unity and both loving and obeying Jesus. For Westerners who are imbued with the spirit of individualism, whether charismatic or not, this emphasis on the importance of the community is very important to understanding the Gospel of John.

It is also crucial to note here that obeying Jesus is not an advocacy for legalism. Obeying the command of Jesus to love one another can hardly be viewed in terms of a series of legalistic rules. Loving both God and others is a basic way of life and is different than merely keeping a set of rules. Loving Jesus represents a commitment to copying the way of Jesus. I would add that because the world does not know God, the way of the Spirit might appear to those in the world as though a Christian may be following a set of legalistic rules (14:17).

I would also remind you not to become overly concerned about how we address our prayers, namely, whether we pray to God or in the name of

---

113 This text likely means that the Counselor would be a substitute for Jesus. But great care must be taken lest one thinks that the Spirit's direction would be different from that of Jesus. Such an idea would be contrary to another of the Paraclete sayings.
114 G. Borchert, *John 12–21*, 120.

Jesus (14:14; 15:7, 16). Westerners tend to think in terms of making precise word-distinctions in the Godhead, whereas the Semites thought more holistically and in word-pictures.[115] Accordingly, when Jesus indicates that he will send "another Counselor," it is hardly a stretch to view Jesus as the disciples' first Counselor.

I should mention here some problem interpretations of this text. The suggestion of some Muslim writers that the other counselor is Mohammed is a very fanciful construct.[116] The proposal, however, by some well-meaning Christians that there are two stages of experiencing the Holy Spirit is also a construct, based on the evangelist's statement that the Counselor has been living "with" you and will be "in" you. There is no warrant for suggesting that the storyteller is making such a distinction. The Greek prepositions "with" (*para*) and "in" (*en*) hardly carry that weight. The Greek, however, can carry a temporal distinction or two different relationships. The text probably means that the disciples were experiencing God *with them* in Jesus (their "Emmanuel," cf. Matt 1:23) and the promise was that the Spirit would be coming to be *in them*—or as the evangelist later recounts that Jesus breathed on them and said, "Receive the Holy Spirit" (John 20:22).[117]

Now, this expected Spirit is also labeled as the Spirit of Truth, which coordinates with the nature of both God and Jesus (1:16, 8:31-32, 14:6) and is contrasted with the way of the devil—the one who is clearly designated as a liar, in whom no truth exists! I repeat: lying is the way of the devil, and Christians are warned that liars are children of the devil and have the spirit of antichrist (8:44; cf. 1 John 2:26). Living with or in the Spirit, therefore, means living with or in the truth and contrary not only to the way of the devil but also to the way of the world and its self-serving perspectives (14:17).

The mention of the world leads the storyteller back to the anxiety and loneliness of the disciples and their concern over being orphaned by the departure of Jesus. In response, Jesus informs them that he will not leave them abandoned but will come to them (14:18). He does not tell them that he will

---

115 See my "Excursus 16: John's Gospel on the Trinity" in G. Borchert, *John 12–21*, 117–18.

116 For my discussion of some Muslim interpretations of "another Counselor" as being Mohammed, see G. Borchert, *John 12–21*, 120–121.

117 I would also suggest that as we read the New Testament, we take great care when interpreting English texts not to assume that expressions of one Greek writer necessarily mean the same thing in another Greek writer. Always remember that the Johannine writer does not use chronology in the same way that Luke does.

not depart, but that his departure will only be for a little while (14:19) and after the "little while" their reality will greatly change. They will then understand that "I am in the Father," "You are in me," and "I am in you."

While these words probably confuse the disciples at first,[118] Jesus is attempting to alert them to what lies ahead. When he says the one who loves me and "keeps my commandments" will be loved by the Father, he likewise does not mean that someone can earn their way to acceptance with God. Instead, it reflects the close relationship Christians have with the Father through Jesus. Then the statement concludes with the promise that Jesus will manifest himself to them (14:21). The great hope of the people of God is to see God. In the Old Testament, theophanies (experiences of God) were normally accompanied by a sense of fear (cf. Gideon in Judg 6:22 and Isaiah in Isa 6:5). But Jesus is intimating that a new era is dawning when no fear is suggested (cf. 1 John 4:18, where fear and love are contrasted).

Even more intriguing is the fact that Jesus closes this first Paraclete saying by indicating that he and the Father will come and make their home/resting place (*monēn/monai*) with the faithful disciples (14:23). What a promise! At the beginning of chapter 14, Jesus indicated that he would be "going away" to prepare resting places for the disciples (*monai*; 14:1), but now he is saying that he and the Father are "coming" to have their resting place (*monēn*) in the disciples. What a story! Is that idea not an awesome thought? With this understanding in mind, it is time to turn to the second Paraclete statement.

This pericope begins by reminding the reader that the time is advancing to the death of Jesus, but he is still with the disciples. Then the evangelist again introduces the Paraclete (*paraklētos*), but this time he refers to the full name of this divine *persona* as the "Holy Spirit" (used only three times in John [14:26; cf. 1:23, 20:22] and not in the Johannine epistles or Revelation). Is the evangelist trying to emphasize one of the Spirit's role to remind and interpreting the teaching of Jesus here? It is a fascinating thought because he also states that the Spirit was sent by the Father "in my name." When we remember that the teaching of Jesus represents the teaching of God (7:17, 28; 8:28), then there is a clear harmony in the messages that come from the three *personae* of God. The early Christians had not yet defined the concept of

---

118 Note that the evangelist indicates that one of the disciples who was in this conversation was named Judas (not Iscariot). This Judas is not otherwise identified. For some possibilities, see G. Borchert, *John 12–21*, 129 and R. Brown, *John*, 2. 541.

the triune God (Trinity), but the Johannine community was working on that task.[119]

We can say with some degree of confidence that the storyteller would generally resist any suggestions that the coming of the Spirit would warrant the delivering of a new or changed message. He would probably affirm that one of the Spirit's roles would be to remind Christ's followers of what Jesus said or implied.[120] The evangelist certainly would have resisted any ideas being projected that the Spirit would supply a new set of laws. But the Spirit could assist in the reinterpretation of the Old Testament—but only if those interpretations followed the pattern Jesus used. The storyteller would also have resisted any changes to the *kerygma* (the main elements of the gospel preaching). But he probably would have cautiously accepted Christians' growing insights into the implications of the gospel—if they harmonized with the perspectives of Jesus.

The evangelist moves to bring these introductory statements concerning the Paraclete to a conclusion by using the Semitic greeting and farewell "Peace!" (*shalom*), which had been familiar to all Jews since the Aaronic benediction (Num 6:26). The term "peace" was used to symbolize the new order under Roman domination as the *pax Romana*, but the "new order" with Jesus is to mean "peace" in the world "under God."[121]

With these words of farewell ("peace") in mind, Jesus again returns to the anxiety of the disciples and seeks to calm their fears and troubles concerning his departure. He acknowledges that he is going away, but he also adds that he is coming back to them, and they should rejoice that he is going to the Father who is preeminent (John 14:28).

It is indeed a farewell message, and is given to assure the disciples that Jesus understands their fears—their reality—before he leaves the scene. The awareness that Jesus knows what they will face should help the disciples believe in him and also approach the unknown, but then the evangelist adds that Jesus also understands the reality of evil and the power of the evil one who

---

119 For a discussion of the early church's wrestling with defining the role of Jesus as compared to their more than two centuries' attempt at defining the role of the Spirit—and it still is not settled—see G. Borchert, *Tension*, 80–85.

120 Schnackenburg has argued that the Spirit's role "simply continues Jesus' revelation, not by providing new teachings, but only by taking what Jesus himself 'taught' to a deeper level" (*St. John*, 3. 83.).

121 See G. Borchert, *John 12–21*, 133 and E.C. Hoskyns, *The Fourth Gospel*, ed. T.N. Davey (London: Faber & Faber, 1956), 461.

seeks to dominate the world. While the evil one's power is strong, Jesus assures the disciples that it is impossible for that "ruler of this world" to dominate or control Jesus. Knowing the power of Jesus and his relationship to the Father should, therefore, give the disciples (and later Christians) a sense of confidence for living in the world (14:29-31).

(The evangelist seems to indicate that Jesus told them, "Rise, let us go." These words are clearly a terminal statement for the discussion, but they do not quite fit the present context and the organization of this gospel. Many scholars have struggled to give sense to them, but I have yet to read a convincing rationale for their presence in the current context of the gospel. Accordingly, I prefer to treat them either as an unedited conclusion to an oral pericope or as an earlier unedited version of John's story that in the present construction of the gospel does not now quite fit.)

These first two segments of the reflections on the Paraclete or Spirit passages are now complete, and they await the final three segments after we deal with the *mashal* of the vine and the branches.

The Centerpiece of the Farewell Cycle: The *Mashal* of the Vine and the Branches (15:1-25)[122]

The centerpiece of the Farewell Cycle is one of the strategic texts in John's gospel. It elaborates on the issues introduced in the foot-washing scene (13:1-20) and brings to focus the message of the new command of Jesus (13:34-35) through the picturesque descriptions in the second of John's magnificent *mashals*.[123] The superb artistry or picture-thinking ability of the storyteller is on display for everyone to witness in chapter 15. But there is far more here than one might find on first reading.

In this *mashal*, Jesus is portrayed in the final set of expanded "I am" sayings[124] as the foundational vine (15:1, 5), and his Father is viewed as the vinedresser

---

122 For a summary of how scholars divide the text, see G. Borchert, *John 12–21*, 137, fn. 194.

123 As I indicated earlier, I have chosen to use the term *mashal* rather than parable because of A. Julicher's restrictive idea that a parable should have one main point. See the excellent work of Craig Blomberg, *Interpreting the Parables* (Downers Grove, IL: InterVarsity, 1990).

124 There are two final *egō eimi* ("I am") sayings in which Jesus identifies himself to the arresting band (18:5-6). Contrast Jesus' self-identification here with Peter's later two denials (*ouk eimi*—"I am not") at 18:17, 25.

or farmer who does the trimming or pruning. Followers of Jesus are pictured as the shoots or branches that grow on the main vine. The Father's role is to prune the branches to ensure they stay healthy. The role of the branches, however, is to make sure they stay attached to the vine for sustenance or life. The basic assumption is that the branches are in the vine and have already been made acceptable (clean). But for the branches to remain fruitful, they must continue to be attached to Jesus—to abide in the vine (15:3).[125]

The branches may be tempted to misunderstand who they are, thinking they are the vine (like Adam and Eve in the Garden) and can sustain themselves (be self-sufficient) without reference to the vine (their source of sustenance from God). Getting confused on this issue, however, is the recipe for doom because Jesus says, "apart from me, you can do nothing" (15:5). For a branch to become detached from the vine means that the branch will wither and be cut from the vine. Thus, it will end in the fire pit (15:6). (I would remind you that this text functions as a counterbalance to the statement of security in 10:28-30. In contexts of freedom and choice, the New Testament writers often issue warnings.[126])

Staying attached is the answer to removal (the counterbalance to an over-emphasis on security). Heeding the warning and remaining attached to the vine (Jesus) is the secret to being fruitful. These Christians have a living relationship with Jesus (and with the Father) who sustains them in life (15:7). They are the ones who glorify God as tested and proven disciples (15:8).

Do you recall what glorifying God means for Jesus in this gospel? Is John getting serious? Yes, following Jesus may be very demanding. But this text tells us that these faithful branches (disciples) are loved by the Lord, follow his ways, and are filled with his joy (15:9-11). An intriguing picture of authentic discipleship is unfolding here. The focus is not simply on the initial event of coming to believe in Jesus (becoming a Christian), but on the long-range need for a sustaining relationship in the vine (Jesus). Such a relationship enables believers to overcome the temptation that comes to all humans who suppose

---

125 Israel is pictured as a vine, which is God's concern in the Old Testament (see, e.g., Ps 80:8-9, Isa 27:2-5, Ezek 17:1-10, Hos 10:1). But disobedient Israel is pictured as a wild vine (Jer 2:21) or a dried/withering vine that is ready for the fire: see e.g., Ezek 15:1-8, 19:10-14. Josephus indicated that a golden cluster of grapes adorned the Herodian Temple representing Israel (*Antiquities* 15.11.3 and *Wars* 5.5.4)

126 This text often leads scholars to debate the issue of security, but I have maintained that the primary issue is fruitfulness rather than security. For an example of the debate, see D. Carson, *John*, 515 and B. Witherington, *John's Wisdom*, 258.

they can become self-sustaining. Christians need the continuing support of God: Choosing the other route leads to tragedy.

As we reread John's gospel, we cannot help but realize that many people believed in Jesus but later abandoned him and turned to their own ways (cf. 6:66). The desire to be the decision-makers, to be in control, to presume to be the vine—not branches (15:5)—means a replay of the Garden of Eden story (cf. Gen 3:3). For the Johannine storyteller, authentic discipleship means staying attached to the vine and producing fruit as the result of that attachment.

Having pictured discipleship in this manner, the storyteller next turns to a reconsideration and expansion of the "New Commandment" he introduced in 13:34-35.[127] But notice that "loving one another" now means being willing "to lay down [one's] life"—to die—for others (15:13). This expansion places Jesus' earlier words in a far more intensive setting. Now the command to love could easily demand one's life.

(We may joyfully sing "They will know we are Christians by our *love*." But would we be willing to sing, "They will know we are Christians by our *death*"? What do you think of that idea as a motto for life? I suggest that we ponder that change seriously because it involves far more than mere words. It is not easy to accept because it changes the entire base system of our thinking about love. Moreover, I would not want you to forget that these words are given in this context of the Farewell Cycle when Jesus is preparing the disciples for his death. This statement is not part of a fairytale: it is a story about suffering and death, about dealing with evil and hatred. But thankfully, it is also about hope and new life.)

Although Jesus is talking about his departure, he is also thinking about what will come after his death: he changes from calling the disciples "servants" to calling them "friends" (15:14-15).[128] He wants them to know what is about to happen, and his goal is that they will bear fruit and that their work will have lasting implications. Indeed, he wants them to know that he "chose" them, and he wants them to have access to the Father in or through "his name"

---

127 Those who attempt to make distinctions between *phileō* and *agapaō* in ch. 21 (which I will treat at that point) should understand that there is a fascinating play on those two verbs at this point also. The Greek words behind "friends" here are both a participial and a noun derived from the verb *phileō*. I doubt that Jesus would have made the distinctions I hear often made by Christians concerning brotherly and self-giving "love." And please remember that Jesus may have been using Aramaic/Hebrew rather than Greek in his conversations anyway.
128 See the previous footnote.

because a difficult future awaits them, and that is the reason he gave them the unrevoked command—to love one another (15:16-17). Jesus knows that the lives of the disciples will not be easy. The world clearly hates him (15:25), and it will hate them too (15:15).[129] The world has persecuted Jesus, their Lord, and they will also experience persecution (15:18-20). The reason for the coming persecution is simple: The persecutors do not know either Jesus or the Father who sent him. But the coming of Jesus has sealed their sin/guilt and left them with no excuse (15:21-23).

The seriousness of the coming persecution thus brings this centerpiece of the Farewell Cycle to a screeching conclusion and returns our attention immediately to the disciples' immanent need for the presence of the Paraclete, the Spirit, in their lives.

Facing the Hostile World and the Final Three Paraclete/Spirit Passages (15:26–16:15)

One of my former professors at Princeton, Dr. Bruce Metzger, delighted in telling students that the chapters and verses in the Bible are about as logical as a rider putting a dot in the text every time the horse bounces in trotting or galloping. Well, in the transmission of this current text the Christian scribe did not place a major mark in the text at 15:26 as beginning a new subsection, but I have chosen to do so.

The storyteller introduces the coming persecution of the disciples with a firm pronouncement of "Guilty!" on the unjustifiable hatred of Jesus and his followers (15:25) in the rearview window. Then he moves forward to the third Paraclete passage at 15:26 by indicating that Jesus will soon send the Counselor, the Spirit of truth, from the Father in his name to bear an authentic witness to him in the world and to assist his chosen disciples with their testimonies concerning him.[130]

---

129 The evangelist supports this phenomenon of being hated without a reason with a reference to Pss 35:19 and 69:4. For a discussion of the use of the Old Testament in supporting ideas in the New Testament, see F. Feed, *Old Testament Quotations in the Gospel of John* (Leiden: Brill, 1965), esp. 94–95.

130 This verse in John has been the subject of a great controversy between churches in the East and the West that centers on the *filioque* ("and the Son") clause in the Nicene Creed. The Orthodox churches argued that the Spirit proceeded from the Father only, while the Roman churches argued that the Spirit proceeded from both the Father "and the Son." This argument has not been settled. For my further comments on this topic, see G. Borchert, *Tension*, 80–84.

The seriousness of the situation for the disciples is indicated by the fact that Jesus sees an urgent need for defending and protecting his followers from being treated as a scandal or becoming scandalized (*skandalisthēte*) in the eyes of the judging world (16:1). This verse has been rendered into English in various ways from being "led into sin" or "falling away" or "committing apostasy." However one may translate this scandalizing of the disciples, the danger to their integrity is clear.

(I do not intend here to belabor the issue of security that causes many Christians anxiety. Some Christians prefer to read over passages such as 1 Corinthians 9–10 and Hebrews 6 and 10 and not take them seriously, for fear that the texts may apply to them. But those texts are in the Bible, and I continue to remind my students and others that the purpose of Jesus and the New Testament writers was not condemnation. Yet we all must take the warnings of the Bible to heart and remember that John, Paul, and others wrote the warnings to prevent Christians from "falling" or turning away from Jesus [e.g., 1 Cor 9:27, 10:11]. I would also remind anxious persons that there are usually statements of assurance or encouragement in those texts that must be coordinated with the warning texts.[131] But taking the biblical warnings seriously, just as Jesus did, is our assigned duty.)

The storyteller, who had lived in the dark period of persecution during the latter part of the first century, personally understood that the threat of persecution and denying the Lord was very real. His mention of excommunications from synagogues and of non-Christians thinking they were justified in arranging for (or being instrumental in) the death of Christians remained a vivid reality. That is the reason for the warning of Jesus here (John 16:2-4a; cf. Mark 13:11-13).

With hardly time to take a breath between paragraphs, the storytelling evangelist launches into the introduction to the fourth Paraclete passage by indicating that Jesus could not detail the dark picture earlier. But now that he is departing and the disciples are grieving as a result, he must spell out why it is advantageous for him to leave so that the Paraclete can come (16:4b-7).

Although this fourth Paraclete message is a masterpiece of brevity, it is also a jewel of enlightened wisdom in the way it spells out for the disciples precisely how the coming of the Spirit will impact their presence and task in the world.

---

131 Please consult my earlier work on the balance of assurance and warning texts in Gerald L. Borchert, *Assurance and Warning* (Nashville: Broadman, 1987).

The Spirit will actively engage the unbelieving world in three major ways. It will convince the world of the nature and reality of sin. Humans on their own may not be able to bring that reality home to other humans, but challenging humans with sin is the special role of the Spirit. How does the Spirit accomplish that task? That question is answered by the Spirit's second function: to remind humans of God's standards of "righteousness." When those standards are made evident, humans then should be able to see more clearly that they do not measure up to God's standards and the Spirit then can easily render the divine judgment on humanity (16:8-11).

The astute reader of this message should quickly realize that we are here dealing with the forensic role of the Spirit. We as mere humans can be used by God, but we must recognize that ultimately the conviction of sin and judgment is not actually the role of humans. We may serve as intermediaries for God in setting up divine-human encounters, but the task of reconciliation and transformation and of condemnation and divine punishment is and always will be the work of God. Humans who misunderstand their role and appropriate to themselves these functions of forgiveness and condemnation are, in fact, idolaters and will meet the scorn of heaven (16:8-11).

Once again we move breathlessly, without pause, to the fifth and final Spirit passage. The storyteller knows that it is impossible to deal with all the matters pertaining to the role of the Spirit in the lives of the disciples, but he has one more encompassing message for them: The Spirit will serve as their guide into all truth. For some interpreters, such as J. Beker, this text may suggest that the Spirit will unveil more truth and, therefore, seem to run counter to the earlier role of the Spirit as a reminder of past information shared by Jesus (14:26).[132] But we are not talking here about secular knowledge—such as astrophysical or micro-processed genetic information. We are focused on life-defining knowledge in relating to God, others, and our reality.

Anyone who has been on a trek into the unknown acknowledges the need for a reliable guide and the foolishness of relying on mere instincts. Trusting in a finely-tuned GPS, even if it may seem to be leading in a circuitous route, is far safer than simply relying on the course of the sun. We all want a guide that understands the lay of the land and knows the roadblocks in our path.

While speaking of the role of Spirit may seem to be quite subjective, the storyteller has tried to suggest a couple of parameters to ensure greater

---

132 See, e.g., J. Beker, *Das Evangelium des Johannes* (Gütersloh: G. Mohn, 1979–81) 2.498.

certainty in the assistance we receive. Answering a couple of questions may point one forward: Is the message consistent with the earlier authority, or is it something quite different? Does the message glorify God, or is it self-serving? These caveats may not seem sufficient, but when all five of the Spirit sayings are combined, they offer a consistent understanding of the role of the Spirit in the life of a Christian. And this statement leads us back to the concern over anxiety and loneliness.

Confronting Anxiety and Loneliness with Jesus: The Great Reversal (16:16-33)

When the storyteller returned to Jesus' earlier refrain of a double "little while," the disciples in exasperation challenged him to explain what he meant (14:16-18). Then with another double *amēn* oath-like saying, Jesus likened the situation to both the sorrow and joy a woman experiences in labor and childbirth. After the child is born, Jesus indicated, the woman is enabled to forget or move beyond the painful anguish of the birthing process (14:20-21). The present anguish or anxiety of the disciples should be viewed similarly because when they see Jesus again, their later joys will extinguish their earlier sorrows. Their doubts will be resolved, and their earlier questions answered.

Then, in another double *amēn* saying, Jesus repeats the promise that praying to the Father in the name of Jesus will bring a divine response (16:23-24; cf. 14:13, 15:16). Indeed, the time of greater clarity is on the horizon when the disciples will understand better about their prayers and the relationship of Jesus and his departure to the Father (14:25-28). They are currently in the strange period of the interim, however.

The disciples respond that they now understand his meaning. But Jesus fires back a question: "Do you *now* believe?" Then to their shock, he counters their pseudo-confidence by telling them that although they are troubled because he is departing, in reality they are about to be scattered and will abandon him. It is a complete reversal of their thinking! And in contrast to their fearful sense of aloneness and anxiety, the storyteller wants his readers to understand that the Father will never abandon Jesus (16:31-32). His relationship to the Father is absolutely secure.

[I must pause here briefly because of some fuzzy thinking I have encountered concerning the well-known cry of dereliction from the cross: "My God, My God, why have you forsaken me?" in Mark (15:34) and Matthew

(27:46).[133] In response to the idea that God could not look on Jesus while he was bearing our sin, I would respond as follows:

- First, this cry should not be treated as a prayer, but rather as an exclamation or a shout of great anguish. Prayers of Jesus in the Gospels normally begin with the Greek word *Pater* ("Father").
- Second, Raymond Brown has shown that this cry in Mark and Matthew is a free Aramaic rendering of the Hebrew in Psalm 22 and was not meant to be understood as a direct quote.[134] Therefore, attempting to suggest that the gospel writers were seeking to use the anguish call as a victory statement of Jesus—as some preachers have done—by referring to the way the psalm ends is at best a very speculative view of that psalm.
- Third, attempting with Albert Schweitzer to use this cry in the gospel as a basis for doing a psychological analysis of Jesus and attempting to picture him as a despairing, eschatological misfit in society lacks credulity.[135]
- Fourth, arguing that the God and Father of Jesus was some type of "stoic-like-god" who lacked passion and was unconcerned while the Son was suffering on the cross is a cruel theological construct that is more like the portrait of the abominable, fire-consuming Moloch than the *Hesed*-loving YHWH of the Old Testament.

If someone asks where was God when Jesus was suffering, the best answer is that God was suffering with Jesus. The suffering of Jesus was very real, but the suffering for the non-abandoning God was also very real. Whatever your theology may be, please do not divide God from Jesus on the cross. Such attempts have resulted in deviant perspectives about God and should themselves be totally abandoned. God loved Jesus and would not abandon him in favor of the world (see 16:32, 3:16). God's love is consistent!

---

133 For my expanded statement on this subject, see G. Borchert, *John 12–21*, 181–83. This cry of dereliction is not mentioned in Luke or John.

134 See Raymond Brown, *The Death of the Messiah: From Gethsemane to the Grave* (New York: Doubleday,1994), 2. 1051–53.

135 Albert Schweitzer, *The Psychiatric Study of Jesus* (Boston: Beacon, 1948) and *The Quest for the Historical Jesus* (New York: Macmillan, 1854), 386, 499–401, etc.

Now, not only is God consistent, but so is Jesus. That is the reason he is concerned for the well-being of the disciples. He reminds them that in the days to come when they face anxiety, they should call upon God, the Father, and make their requests known in the name of Jesus.[136] The Father will hear and answer their concerns (16:26-28; cf.14:13, 15:7). So, again Jesus promises them his departing "peace" (16:33; cf. 14:27). That endowment is not a transitory, vacuous statement. Jesus knows that in the world the disciples will be bombarded with troubles, but his assertion of "peace" here means that the divine presence is with them and will enable them to overcome the hatred and turmoil in the world (16:33).

With this note, the Farewell Cycle has thus come almost full circle. What remains is the final model act of Jesus: his magisterial prayer.

Interpreting the Majestic Model Prayer of Jesus (17:1-26)

As we reach the conclusion to the Farewell Cycle, I would note again that many interpreters in the past have championed the idea that chapters 13–17 should be known as Farewell Discourses. I find that designation too limiting, because there is here a powerful storyline that is often missed. Jesus, here as in the start of the Farewell Cycle, provides a closure to the section with another model of discipleship for his followers: the model prayer, which I believe has been brilliantly developed in seven parts.

While the Synoptic Gospels focus on the Gethsemane prayer of Jesus as the preparatory event before his arrest (Mark14:32-43, Matt 26:36-46, Luke 22:39-46), this magnificent Johannine prayer on first view may seem to provide few connectors to the rest of the gospel story. But please do not judge the storyteller too quickly. This prayer is an amazing piece of literature and serves as a significant summary of the story and an introduction to the Death Story that comes next.

Following a simple, vague introduction ("After Jesus had said these things, he lifted his eyes to heaven"), the storyteller uses the typical word for signaling a prayer: *pater* ("Father"). Then, when he adds the crucial words "the hour

---

136 D. Carson (*John*, 545) notes that two different verbs for "asking" are used here, and he seeks to make a distinction between them. I would simply say that interpreters must be very careful and not try to make distinctions where they are unnecessary. Contrast R. Brown, *John*, 2. 722–23.

has come," we should sense the beginning of an important addition to the Johannine storyline (17:1). Therefore, this prayer clearly provides a magnificent conclusion to the Farewell Cycle as it moves the reader's thought process from the broad spectrum of the coming of Jesus and his message of eternal life through the confrontation with evil and temptation to the Christian summons or task of witnessing, then to the expectation of being with Jesus, and finally to the need for exemplifying the quality of love that should be the life-pattern of the Christian while on earth.

Before moving further into this text, however, I must mention the presence of two Greek verbs, *didonai* ("give") and *apostellein* ("send"), that are used throughout this prayer. They make it abundantly clear that the focus of this prayer is on the mission of Jesus in the establishing of an obedient community that will be composed of faithful representatives of his mission in the world. The community nature of mission in this prayer is thus a crucial theme to grasp here. Otherwise, the reader might turn this prayer chapter into a model for a mystical experience with God.[137]

Having thus introduced the arrival of "the hour," Jesus directs his first petition (17:1-4) to ask that the purposes of God will be completed and that the Father will glorify the Son [with his former glory]. As a result, the Son can bring glory to the Father and to his revelational purposes of "giving" eternal life to all who believe that God "sent" the Son. This first petition uniquely brings to focus the encompassing concerns of the Johannine purpose statement in the coming of Jesus (20:30-31).

The second petition (17:5-8) expands the goal of Jesus' prayer to return to the glory that he had before creation came into existence. Clearly Jesus had been accomplishing the divine purpose for the incarnation—namely, bringing humans to become the children of God by helping them to know and receive the message (*remata*, "words") that the Father had given to Jesus. Those who are familiar with how this gospel begins should quickly recognize that these verses have a close kinship to the content and purpose of John's prologue (1:1-18) and to the importance of "believing," which is the focus of the Cana Cycle (2:1–4:54).

The appearance of the Greek verb *erōtō* ("I pray") signals a major shift in the third and fourth petitions (17:9-18) to the concern for the safety and well-being of the disciples. Jesus is aware that the road ahead for them will be

---

137 See G. Borchert, *John 12–21*, 188.

rough, so the third petition addresses opposition to the gospel. His prayer is not a general one for the world, but a specific one in which we can feel the deep pathos when he calls on the "Holy" (*hagie*) Father to keep his chosen ones unified in the Father's special "name." Moreover, Jesus also reminds the Father that, through his divine name (or presence), he has faithfully preserved all his disciples from disaster—except the devil-man (6:70), the one doomed for destruction (17:12).[138]

But everything is now changing! Jesus is about to return to the Father. So, he longs for the disciples to experience a God-given satisfaction or joy. Yet he knows that the world hates them, so he asks not for their removal from the world but for their protection from the clutches of the evil one (17:15-16). This fourth petition, "Sanctify (*hagioson*) them in the truth!" (17:17), is a prayer for them to be holy; to be a people of integrity; to be a people who fulfill the mission of Jesus. Indeed, his followers are to be like Jesus, who in this context strangely prays that "I might consecrate myself" (*hagiazō*) in order that they might be made holy (*hagiasmenoi*; 17:19).[139]

You may ask why I have emphasized the Greek words for holiness here. The answer is that this *hagios* family of words is very rare in John's gospel. They primarily appear in the third and fourth petitions and in the Festival Cycle (10:36)—where the focus is on the conflicts of Jesus. I do not think that this combination is a mere chance happening. I believe the Johannine story-teller purposely designed this prayer to mirror the storyline of the gospel as it prepares the reader to face the death story of Jesus.

God's mission plan is hardly to send a fleet of rescue planes to evacuate the suffering disciples from the world. That would mean that God is aborting his mission strategy. Instead, God's plan is to send troops into the world as light shines into the darkness for the purpose of accomplishing the divine purposes. So, to conclude this magisterial prayer, we turn to the final three petitions.

The second appearance of *erōtō* signals the second major shift in the prayer (17:20). The focus now moves to the forthcoming mission of Jesus in the Farewell Cycle and to those who will believe throughout the world because of the witness of these disciples.

The fifth petition, therefore, is directed to the need for unity among all believers (17:21) so that "the world might believe" that the Father sent the

---

138 There is a Greek wordplay here on the idea of "perishing" and "perdition" or "destruction"—*apoleto* and *apoleias*.
139 See G. Borchert, *John 12–21*, 200–204.

Son on his mission. It mirrors the earlier concern that Jesus expressed about the need for unity in those first disciples (17:11). This need for unity among the followers of Jesus is modeled on the fundamental oneness of Jesus and the Father and is the basis for the proclamation of the gospel (cf. 14:20). Indeed, the evangelist may be thinking that somehow the glory of God is revealed in the unity of the Father and the Son and the love they exhibit for each other. It is also very likely the reason why love and unity are repeatedly emphasized throughout John's gospel (cf., e.g., 13:34-35) and the Johannine epistles (cf., e.g., 1 John 2:8-9, 3:11-18, 4:7-12).

As we turn to the sixth petition, the focus broadens to include the eschatological perspective of Jesus concerning his mission. His vision for his followers stretches far beyond the cosmic realm: he desires that his followers will be enabled to glimpse or experience the glory of this loving, unified relationship within God that has existed even before time began. Jesus truly wants mortals who believe in him to gain the mind-blowing perception of divine love that exists in God (17:24; cf. 14:1-7).

But the eschaton has not yet arrived: the disciples will still be facing a hostile world that does not know or acknowledge either Jesus or the Father. In that context Jesus begins his seventh and final petition in this majestic prayer with the words, "O Righteous Father" (*pater dikaie*; 17:25). Most Christian readers would probably not pause here because those words sound very familiar, but they were not familiar to the early readers of John. The Greek words in the *dikaios/dikaioun* family appear in one other place in the entire Gospel of John: in the Farewell Cycle at 16:8, in the hostile context of the fourth Paraclete passage where Jesus promises that the Spirit will support the disciples in confronting the world.[140] Do you think this combination might be a chance happening in a carefully constructed prayer? I doubt it.

Some interpreters are frustrated by John's style. Indeed, Leon Morris thinks there is no petition in these verses.[141] He is technically correct. But reread these verses and picture the disciples as the recipients of the Paraclete and their task in confronting a hostile world on behalf of Jesus. Clearly, Jesus loves them and prays that the love of God will be in them (17:26). Then ask yourself: What would be the prayer of Jesus to the "Righteous Father"? Would it not be "Help them to follow me"?

---

140 See G. Borchert, *John 12–21*, 208–10.
141 Leon Morris, *The Gospel According to John*, NICNT (Grand Rapids: Eerdmans, 1995), 652.

In this Farewell Cycle, Jesus demonstrates the true nature of discipleship by washing the feet of his followers. He has dealt with their concerns of loneliness and anxiety over his coming departure; has promised them the coming presence of the Paraclete to support, teach, protect, confront, and guide them; and has illustrated for them in the vine and the branches what it means to live in him. Jesus has prayed for the disciples that they might follow his model of "glory." He has petitioned that they might be protected from evil, might be unified in mission, might anticipate being with him, and might be like him in carrying out the loving mission of God.

Do you now think this prayer might summarize many of the concerns that have been detailed throughout this gospel story? Every time I read this prayer, I stop and ponder the amazing depth of the evangelist's perception. It is as though he has given us a brief glimpse of the heart of Jesus and an overview of the divine purpose in sending Jesus on mission to the world. But now we must turn to the painful cost of that mission: the death story of Jesus.

Chapter 6

Stories Concerning the Death of the King
(18:1–19:42)

The death story of Jesus is without doubt a fascinating piece of literature. I have been repeatedly amazed at how the storyteller could have woven both the positive and negative subplots together and skillfully formed a unique symphony. The Death Story is a prime example of the way in which this gospel is so well constructed that the individual stories fit together into a brilliant narrative. Many of my colleagues and friends who have written commentaries on John cannot countenance the possibility that a Galilean fisherman who had not received a classical education could have penned such a superb artistic work. I gave up trying to convince others about who can and cannot pen such a fascinating, literary jewel. My goal, therefore, has been to focus on what the written gem has to say and how it is said and then thank God for what I can learn from it.[142]

In this segment of the gospel, the storyteller portrays Jesus as fully in control of the events that take place in the narrative. No religious or political figure can compare with him. All his opponents are mere hollow people. Several will become frustrated that they are not in charge of affairs, as they believe they should be. They may threaten, try to influence, and even use force to be in control, but all such attempts only confirm that they are hollow people in comparison to the one person who is about to die and who does not seem to be ruffled by the proceedings.

Also intriguing is the way the subplots are interwoven so that they influence the way the reader is directed to interpret one story by another, and the shifting back and forth also means that all subplots are advancing together. On the other hand, the reader who is familiar with all four gospels and may have internally harmonized the Death Story to include subplots or aspects from all the gospels may wonder: Did the Johannine evangelist purposely omit

---

142 See G. Borchert, *John 12–21*, 214 for a helpful work on the ability of the Johannine evangelist in weaving together the various subplots of the Death Story of this gospel. See also J.P. Heil, *Blood and Water* (Washington: Catholic Biblical Quarterly Monograph Series, 1995).

some segments of the story? Of course, he may not have known some of those aspects of the fuller story, but writing at the end of first century and not in the middle of that century forces one to reflect on those missing elements. For example, John does not mention the following:

- Judas' kiss
- Pilate's washing of his hands
- Simon of Cyrene carrying the cross
- special recognition of the two men crucified with Jesus
- further recognition by Judas of his sin [or ... his death]
- Jesus' cry of abandonment
- the Temple's veil ripping
- the centurion's confession that Jesus was the Son of God
- a guard at the tomb.[143]

But we must remember that in the purpose statement the evangelist tells us he made a conscious choice of the stories he used, selecting all to lead his readers to believe in Jesus so that they might have life in or through him (20:31).

The Chilling Arrest in the Garden (18:1-11)

In the first segment of the Death Story the evangelist deals with three major issues: the move of Jesus and the disciples to the sanctuary of a garden, the coming of Judas with the fully-armed arresting band, and the attempt by Peter to defend Jesus and prevent his arrest.

The narrative begins by linking the Farewell Cycle with its concluding magisterial prayer to this death story by noting that after Jesus has finished speaking, he and his disciples cross the Kidron valley to a garden. Gardens were normally viewed in Jewish tradition as places of peace and tranquility, and the evangelist's geographical description (18:1) would generally fit the traditional site for what is called the Garden of Gethsemane today.[144]

The introduction of Judas in this context is undoubtedly intended by the storyteller to suggest a picture of the confrontation between good and evil

143 G. Borchert, *John 12–21*, 215.
144 For brief descriptions of sites around Jerusalem, see G. Borchert, *The Lands of the Bible*, 1. 56–78.

because Judas, the betrayer, leads a group of soldiers and Temple police[145] to the special place where Jesus has often met with his disciples. In doing so, Judas violates a sacred trust (18:2). The further details concerning this unscheduled meeting only enhance the dark and evil nature and intent of this arresting band: they are pictured with torches and weapons in contrast to Jesus and his disciples (18:3).

When the two groups come face to face, the importance of Judas has already faded into the background, and it is Jesus who steps forward and asks who they are seeking. When they respond "Jesus of Nazareth,"[146] Jesus answers with his awesome self-identification, "I am" (*egō eimi*; 18:5), which we have encountered several times before and that mirrors the self-disclosure of God to Moses (cf. Exod 3:14). But on this occasion what happens next must greatly surprise everyone: the arresting band fall to the ground, as though the forces of evil are confronted by the presence of divine holiness, and for a breathless moment are "undone" and have capitulated (John 18:6).

But the intent of the incarnation is not to overwhelm the evil power structure by sheer force. God's plan is to win mortals by allowing them the freedom to choose obedience over forced acknowledgement. So, after again affirming "I am," Jesus allows even the arresting band the right to arrest him, but he has promised to protect the disciples while he is on earth, so the evangelist quotes the prayer of Jesus as though it is as authoritative as Holy Scripture (18:8-9; cf. 17:12). He then instructs the arresters to release

---

145 I have purposely kept the nature of this arresting band vague because the word that is used to describe the soldiers, *speiran,* could refer to a detachment of up to 600 Roman soldiers. The Jewish members of the arresting band are *hyperetas,* which could refer to various assistants including Temple officers and police. The terms used here do not seem to be employed in their technical meanings. See G. Borchert, *John 12–21,* 217–18. It is difficult to determine who was in charge of this arresting band, but the fact that Jesus was taken to Annas first suggests that the Jews oversaw the arrest. It would be unlikely that Pilate would have been involved early in the arrest and then allowed the arresters to take Jesus to the high priest, but strange things can happen in conquered states between authority figures. Once Jesus was turned over to Pilate, he did not seem to have been returned to the control of the Jews, although Matthew does suggest (Matt 27:65) that there was a working agreement made between them concerning the guard at the tomb. There is no such arrangement in the Gospel of John.

146 The designation "Jesus of Nazareth" is used four times in this gospel: when Philip introduced Jesus to Nathaniel and we learned that Jesus is then designated by Philip as the "King of Israel" and much more (1:45-49), twice in this context of the arrest (18:5, 7), and in the official charge on the cross when Pilate designated him as the "the King of the Jews" (19:19).

the disciples and let them go. When Jesus voluntarily then submits, it is clear who is in control—even of his own arrest.

Yet, one of the disciples thinks he understands the situation better than Jesus and wants to show he is in charge. Dear Peter wants to prove himself as supportive of Jesus, so he draws his puny sword and cuts off the right ear of Malchus, a slave of the high priest. But in so doing, Peter only confirms that he is following the pattern of the arresting mob. Jesus is not prepared to accept that strategy, however. As Matthew suggests, this disciple has no idea of what divine power is like (cf. Matt 26:53). The use of force is not the Jesus way. There is another way, which Jesus is prepared to accept: the cup of sacrifice (John 18:11).

While the other gospels do not identify Peter as the clueless disciple, the Johannine storyteller consistently identifies Peter because it seems as though the beloved disciple and Peter are being compared throughout this gospel. (My suspicion is that there may have been a little friction or "one-upmanship" between the churches that were established by Peter and John [the "other" or "Beloved Disciple"] and that this friction even spilled over into the slightly diminished view of Peter and the elevation of John/the Beloved Disciple in this gospel [see, e.g., some references here at 18:10-11 and in 13:8-10, 23-26, 36-38; 18:15-16, 25-27; 20:2-8; 21:7-8, 15-22].[147] Whether or not my speculation here is viable, we do not know, but we do know that the "one-upmanship" between the Eastern and Western churches grew until it ended in the Great Medieval Schism of Orthodox and Roman churches that continues even to this day.)

The Late-Night Hearings and Peter's Denials
(18:12-27)

The motley group of Jewish arresters bind Jesus and first take him to Annas, the "godfather-like" high priest who was deposed by the Romans as uncooperative. In his place they installed Caiaphas, his son-in-law, who made

---

147 While I do not find the arguments of G. Klein convincing concerning the opposition to Peter in the church being read back in the resurrection stories, some of his thoughts are worth pondering. See "*Die Verleungnung des Petrus. Eine traditionsgeschichtliche Untersuchung,*" ZTK 58 (1961), 285–328.

the fatal decision concerning Jesus (11:50), but Annas technically still holds the title because high priests held their title for life (18:13-14).[148]

To keep the reader informed about the progress of the multiple scenes, however, the storyteller skillfully moves our attention back and forth to keep us aware of the ongoing events.

So, we are back to Peter who seeks to follow Jesus. But unlike the other disciple who is known to the high priest, Peter is forced to stay outside the compound until the other disciple enables him to gain access to the courtyard. Yet when he gains entrance, Peter is quickly questioned about whether he is a disciple of Jesus. His answer stands in stark contrast to the answers of Jesus as he says, "I am not!" (*ouk eimi*; 18:17; cf. the answers of John the Baptizer at 1:20-21). But the storyteller prepares the reader for further revelations as he extends the chill of Jesus' arrest to the shivering Peter who is warming himself around a "charcoal fire" (*anthrakian*; 18:18)—an experience that will later come to haunt him!

Then it is back to the late-night, pseudo-council meeting where Jesus remains serene in his defense by indicating, "I have never done anything in secret." And he actually challenges[149] the high priest with his further statement, "Ask those who heard me!" (18:20-21). Jesus virtually asks, "Where are your witnesses?" It is a direct challenge to the high priest's authority. One of the officers apparently senses that challenge and strikes Jesus for talking back to the high priest. In response, Jesus confronts the man for treating him in such a demeaning manner. Then without further exchange, the high priest sends Jesus to Caiaphas (18:24).

And that conclusion takes us back again to Peter who is still warming himself around the fire. Then those in the circle challenge him with a question: "Are you not also one of his disciples?" Again, Peter answers: "I am not" (*ouk eimi*). But then a colleague of the one who suffered from Peter's sword wound levels a direct counterchallenge to Peter's denial with a stabbing question: "Did

---

148 Annas was installed as high priest by legate Quirinius in 6 AD/CE but was officially removed by Procurator Valerius Gratus (the immediate predecessor of Pilate) in 15 AD/CE, and his son-in-law Caiaphas replaced him. Five other family members also held that post. The Jews finally killed the family that was left when the Temple was destroyed in 70 AD.

149 See G. Borchert, *John 12–21*, 214. For a helpful work on the ability of the Johannine evangelist in weaving together the various subplots of the Death Story of this gospel, see also Heil, *Blood and Water*.

I not see you in the garden with him?" When Peter denies the question again,[150] it is as though the whole world wakes up and shouts their alarm along with the rooster.[151] The other gospels detail that Peter then weeps, but John does not need such a conclusion. Although Peter thought his loyalty was invincible, he has failed the crucial test. The chilling arrest story simply closes in silence.

The Roman Trial and the Scourging of the King
(18:28–19:16)

For the Johannine storyteller, the hasty Jewish late-night hearing is finished and the wrenching denials of Peter are complete. It is time for Pilate to enter the storyline and for the reader to witness a new set of complex subplots.

The scene opens with the Jewish religious hierarchy leading Jesus from the palatial residence of the high priest to the praetorium or judgment hall of the Roman procurator/prefect/governor. Then the evangelist adds the subtle sidenote that the Jewish leadership does not want to become defiled or contaminated by associating with a place where Gentiles live or work and thereby be unable to participate in the sanctity of the Passover.[152] So, to placate the Jewish religious sensitivities, Pilate asks what charge they are filing against Jesus (18:29).[153] When they are vague in their charge, Pilate tells them to dispense with the Roman preliminaries and judge Jesus according to their laws. But the Jews are in no mood simply to be tolerated and therefore inform Pilate that by their Jewish law, Jesus should be put to death and the death should be certified by the Romans (18:32).

---

150 For the extended essay on Peter's denials, see Ernst Haenchen, *John 2* (Philadelphia: Fortress, 1984), 171–74.

151 It is interesting to note that the Romans divided the night watch into four segments, with the third occurring between roughly midnight and 3:00 a.m., the change that they called the "cock crow" (*alectrophonia* or *gallicinium*).

152 The official headquarters of the Roman governor at this time was normally at Caesarea Maritima, but during festivals the governor would normally come to Jerusalem with a full army to prevent uprisings. He could either stay in the Antonio Fortress or in Herod's palace with its three great towers. The judgment seat/room (*Praetorium*) could have been in either place. Contemporary visitors often prefer to think it was in the Antonio Fortress with its *Lithostraton* (the traditional judgment hall and the so-called game room of the soldiers), but Herod's palace may have been more comfortable for the governor.

153 The gardens of Gentile houses were not viewed as contaminated as the living quarters of the Gentiles who were known to abort babies in their homes, a practice despised by Jews.

Their statement gains the governor's attention, and he quickly returns to the praetorium to scrutinize this Jesus and probe the prisoner to try and determine if he really is guilty of treason by pretending to be the "King of the Jews" (18:33). But to Pilate's surprise, Jesus answers his question with another question. (We may wonder if Pilate asked the question without prompting from someone else.) In a sharp response Pilate asks, "Am I a Jew?" Then he continues: "Your own nation delivered you to me. What have you done?" (18:35). (This question should have been asked at the outset of the case!)

The challenge is before Jesus, and he is then ready to answer that his kingdom is not an earthly one. (Scholars have debated the meaning of the terms for kingdom and kingship [*basileialbasileus*] here, but Beasley-Murray is correct that "kingdom" can involve both kingship and kingly reign as *malkuth* would imply in the Hebrew Bible.[154]) If it were simply an earthly kingdom, then Pilate would see a war. But that is not the nature of this kingdom (18:36). Pilate finds that idea intriguing, so he probes Jesus further. "Then you are a King?" Pilate asks. To that question, Jesus responds in the affirmative and then adds that he was born to bear witness to the truth. For a political expedient such as Pilate, that answer is almost humorous, and he probably waves off Jesus and truth with a shrug: "What is truth?" (18:38).

Then the scene returns to the courtyard and the waiting Jews. Pilate must know that simply dismissing the case against Jesus would incite animosity among the Jews, so he devises a clever plan to throw them off-balance. Perhaps he thinks he can gain some popularity points among the people and deliver a punch against those sly religious leaders. So, he tries his scheme. First, he announces that he has found no chargeable offense against this Jesus. But relying on a tradition of releasing one incarcerated villain to the people at the festival of Passover, he offers them a choice: He will give them this strange "King of the Jews" or the nasty villain, Barabbas. Pilate is sure they will choose Jesus. But when the commotion settles, he can hardly believe his ears: they choose the robber, Barabbas (18:40)! For a Roman politician like Pilate, this choice is completely illogical.

So, Pilate must do some recalculating. He leaves the courtyard and retreats to the safety of the praetorium where he has to devise another plan. It is soon forthcoming: he will show those rebellious Jews his determination by having Jesus beaten—perhaps even more than a legitimate condemned

---

154 George Beasley-Murray, *John*, WBC (Waco, TX; Word, 1987), 330–31.

criminal—until he resists no more, and then he will display the emaciated Jesus to all the world.[155] That scheme will show the Jews the reality of Roman authority. Pilate's soldiers are more than happy to follow his wishes. They even put a crown of thorns on Jesus' head and mock him as a petty, local monarch—the "King of the Jews"—and also give Jesus an old purple robe to wear. Pilate is satisfied! So, with a smirk on his face, he brings the grizzly-looking Jesus out to the waiting crowd and declares, "I find no crime in him…Look at him!" (19:1-4).

But to Pilate's surprise, when the religious authorities see sorry-looking Jesus, they lead the people in a rousing chant: "Crucify him!" By this time, Pilate has had enough of this charade and tells them to take Jesus and be responsible for crucifying him. "No! no!" they protest: it's your duty because he broke one of our laws and he ought to die. "He made himself the Son of God!" That charge is completely new to Pilate. The Jews have shifted their complaint to "god-talk," and Pilate has no desire to think about God: God-talk makes him uncomfortable—even afraid (19:8).

Thus, it is back to the praetorium and Pilate addresses Jesus directly: "Where are you from?" But Jesus remains silent. Frustrated, Pilate speaks back to him: "You won't speak to me? Don't you know I have power to release you and to crucify you?" Like night and day, Jesus calmly responds: "You would have no power over me, unless it was given from above." Then he adds that the one who handed him over to Pilate is the worst sinner (19:8-11).

Completely frustrated, Pilate returns to the courtyard and tries to release Jesus. But the sly Jewish leadership still has one "trump card" to play. Pilate's sponsor, Sejanus, is "a Friend of Caesar"—and Pilate desires that same status.[156] The Jews tells Pilate that if he releases Jesus, he is no friend of Caesar. Pilate's will crumbles: he is checked, but not yet checkmated. In an effort

155 It is difficult to know for sure what level of beating is envisaged in this scourging of Jesus. The Romans basically had three levels of whipping: *Justiagatio,* which is akin to lashing; *Flagellatio,* which was severe punishment intended to bring the recipient into submission; and *Verberatio,* which brutalized the victim by using rods and whips with thongs containing bones and metal scraps that were intended to tear the flesh and prepare the person for suffering and death. See my Excursus 21 on "The Roman Scourging of Jesus and His Condition" in G. Borchert, *John 12–21,* 246–48.

156 For my further comments on Aelius Sejanus, see G. Borchert, *John12–21,* 255 and esp. fns. 97 and 98. It would be difficult at this point to determine if the expression "friend of Caesar" was being used technically or as a general term to refer to a supporter of the Roman establishment.

at self-preservation, Pilate brings Jesus out to the public judgment square or "pavement" (Hebrew: *Gabbatha*) and sits down in a formal act to begin the final procedures.

The Johannine storyteller is ready for the verdict. It is high noon (the sixth hour) on the day of Preparation and almost time for the butchers to begin the slaughter of the Passover lambs. Jesus, "the Lamb of God" who will "take away the sin of the world," is at the stand—just as the Baptizer had predicted (1:29). Then Pilate addresses the Jews—and all the world: "Here is your King!" (19:14). It is a decisive moment. The Jews are shouting, "Crucify him!" Then, as time almost stands still and with an air of pseudo-control, Pilate asks the resounding question: "Shall I crucify your King?"

What will be the determining answer? The Jewish high priests then commit their deadly sin. Together they cry, "We have no king but Caesar" (19:15)—a cry that could rattle the stout doors of *Sheol* and likely cause the ancient prophet Samuel to jump out of the grave (cf. 1 Sam 8:4-9); a cry that violates everything Samuel represented. It is inconceivable that the high priests of the Jewish people would utter such words. Did God not want to be the king in Israel (cf. Judg 8:23, Isa 26:13)? These religious leaders have completely compromised their roles as the representatives of God in order to grasp control. Surely that is not a familiar pattern among the people of God—or is it?

This segment in the death story of Jesus is thus finished. Pilate hammers the case "Closed!" and delivers (*paredōken*) Jesus to be crucified (19:16).[157]

---

157 The statement does not mean that Pilate gave the authority to the Jews for crucifying Jesus. In the mind of the evangelist, Pilate was still considered to be in charge of the verdict on the death sign or *titlon* (19:22), and he was still in control of the disposal of the bodies (19:38). It here simply means that the crucifiers were now in charge of crucifying Jesus but that Pilate managed the process. R. Brown (*The Death of the Messiah*, 1.855) categorizes this statement by the evangelist as "careless narrative style," but he may be a bit picky at this point.

The Crucifixion of the King
(19:17-37)

When the next segment of the Death Story begins, Jesus is being led to Skull-hill (*Golgotha*) carrying his own cross piece.[158] There he is crucified between two other men. The description of the crucifixion in John is quite brief and lacks the longer descriptions in the Synoptic Gospels that gave rise to the traditional idea of the *Via Dolorosa* ("Way of Sorrows") and the multiple "stations of the cross" with weeping women and Simon of Cyrene carrying the cross (cf. Mark 15:21, Matt 27:32, Luke 23:26).

[I pause here to mention that because Hadrian destroyed and rebuilt Jerusalem as Aelia Capitolina in the early part of the second century, it is difficult to be certain concerning the location of sites mentioned in the Gospels. But the traditional site of Skull-Hill as being under the site of the Church of the Holy Sepulcher has more historical support than some other places. The site called Gordon's Calvary, or the Garden Tomb, is a peaceful setting for reflecting on the death and resurrection of Jesus. But it lacks the historical support that goes back to the time of Queen Helena with the Christianizing of the empire, the building of churches, and the identification of holy sites that followed Constantine. The pockmarked hill near the Garden tomb, however, does offer an excellent example of what a "skull-hill" could originally have been like since it is impossible to visualize the tomb and the site of the crucifixion at the Church of the Holy Sepulcher.[159]]

The crucifixion takes place near the city so that the offense of Jesus stated on the *titlon*—as "Jesus of Nazareth, the King of the Jews"—is seen by many people. Indeed, because the officers have written it in Hebrew, Latin, and Greek (the languages of the conquered people, the conquerors, and of business throughout the empire), the message is widely understood. But when the high priests protest and demand that Pilate should change the offense to a mere "claim" to be the King of the Jews, the governor is hardly in the mood for

---

158 For the process of crucifixion, see my Excursus 23 "The Crucifixion of Jesus' in G. Borchert, *John 12–21*, 263–64. Briefly I would note that crucifixion could take place in four forms: on an "X" cross, on a single pole with the hands fastened above the head, on a T-shaped cross where the cross piece would fit into a notch at the top, and on a pole where the cross piece would fit in a notch lower down the pole.
159 For additional information, see G. Borchert, *John12–21*, 262–63.

yielding to the religious manipulators. So, the *titlon* remains as the official written proclamation.

While the storyteller keeps the crucifixion story very brief, he does emphasize several important points both around the cross and later in the death of "the King." Concerning the picture around the cross, he highlights two groups as a study in vivid contrast.

The first group, a squad (*quaternion*) of uninterested soldiers who are busy profiting from the victims' few possessions—in this case their clothing—divide most of the possessions of Jesus, but they do not want to tear his seamless tunic (*chiton*). So, they cast lots for it (19:24) and in so doing the storyteller sees their action as a fulfilment of Ps. 22:18, but with a slightly different meaning than is conveyed in that psalm.[160]

The second group involves the friends of Jesus who are deeply concerned about their friend and mourn his torturous death. This group is composed of what seems to be four women (three of whom are likely named Mary, one being the mother of Jesus) and a man who could be the storyteller. Then in what appears to be some of his final wishes, Jesus says to his mother: "Woman, here is your son!" To the man in the group, Jesus says: "Here, is your mother!" Then the writer adds: "from that time/hour on the disciple took her into his home" (John 19:27).

[Normally this type of statement from the oldest son to his mother would be regarded as the equivalent of a testamentary instruction, and the new son would be given charge of the mother. But as Beasley-Murray has clearly stated, some Roman Catholic and other interpreters have completely reversed that idea and placed the disciple under the care of Mary.[161] The church, in this type of thinking, was then likewise assigned to the care of Mary, symbolically evocative of the lady Zion, who after the birth pangs brings forth a new people in joy.[162]]

In turning to the death of Jesus, the Johannine storyteller highlights several other crucial issues. The first involves Jesus' sense of "thirst" (*dipsō*),

---

160 Note that the Hebrew text is a two-line, poetic, synonymous parallelism. But even though they both involve disposing of Jesus' clothes, the evangelist has split the two lines to focus on two different actions by the soldiers.

161 See Beasley-Murray, *John*, 349–50 and Contra D. Unger, "The Meaning of John 19:26-27 in the Light of Papal Documents," *Mirianum* 21 (1959), 186–221.

162 For a slight variation on this view, see R. Brown, *John*, 2. 925. For my further comments on these ideas, see G. Borchert, *John 12–21*, 269.

which introduces the theme of everything "being finished" or "coming to a conclusion" (*tetelestai/teleiōthē*)—a theme that is rare in this gospel but appears three times in John 19:28-30 and twice in the great prayer of Jesus (17:4, 23). The King is dying (cf. the similar idea in the Marcan Death Story), and the suffering of Jesus is viewed as connected to the anguish expressed in Psalms 22 and 69 (see especially "thirst" in 69:3, 21). But the focus in John quickly moves from tasting the sour wine to the work of Jesus being completed in the expression, "It is finished"—*tetelestai* (Greek) and *Consummatum est* (Latin)— a theme that has been repeated countless times throughout Christian history and that the Johannine Seer announced would be echoed at the end of time (Rev 16:17, 21:6).

Jesus then bows his head and releases his spirit ("delivered" or "handed over" [*paredōken*], 19:30). The Greek verb *paradidōmi* has been used many times and particularly in this second part of the Johannine gospel, but up to this point it has carried a haunting theme of betrayal and condemnation. Now in this death scene it is employed to assert that Jesus has been in control throughout the story—even to his last breath. The forces of evil may have schemed and manipulated people and events to control the story, but ultimately the obedient Son of God followed the directions of the Father and chose the time of his death. Then the storyteller reminds us again that it is the day of Preparation—the day for the killing of the Passover lambs; the day when the Lamb of God would initiate the process of "[taking] away the sin of the world" (19:31; cf. 19:14, 1:29).

Although the Roman authorities would usually leave bodies on crosses for some time—even allowing birds and animals an opportunity to pick at the bodies—as an example to potential rebels not to follow the patterns of those being crucified and to ensure that crucified criminals had in fact died, in this particular year Nisan 14 is the day before a high Sabbath. Therefore, the religious authorities request that the land be purified before Sabbath and that the bodies be removed from crosses before sunset (cf. Deut 21:22-23). Pilate agrees that the soldiers should administer the *crucifragium* (the breaking of the legs) to ensure that breathing of those dying would cease and a quick death would thus follow.[163] The soldiers comply with the order for the two other men who were crucified along with Jesus, but when they come to Jesus, they find

---

163 For further information on the *crucifragium*, see G. Borchert, *John 12–21*, 274, esp. fn. 153, and other sources there.

that he is already dead. So, they do not need to use the heavy cudgel to break his legs. Yet, to make sure that Jesus is dead, one of the soldiers uses his spear and opens a large wound in the side of Jesus (19:31-33).

But what happens next is obviously a surprise that has left biblical interpreters scrambling to explain. Moreover, it has created considerable debate among scholars concerning the symbolic significance of the event. When the spear pierces the side of Jesus, according to a witness, blood and water flow forth (19:34). This sight of "blood and water" is clearly regarded as a significant sign. (The witness to the event virtually took an oath to declare his testimony as true.)

There are many theories concerning this phrase of "blood and water." As I have earlier indicated,[164] some scholars have suggested that instead of the side being pierced, the upper pericardial sac was punctured, which resulted in separate blood and water bursting forth.[165] A less convincing view is that the separated mixture filled the lungs and rib cage, and the membrane was punctured.[166] But most physical explanations still leave us a little baffled.

(The pictorial view that in some way represents the bleeding heart of Jesus in the thought of the evangelist is intriguing but not very viable. Yet I should mention a movie representation that I saw years ago that pictured Jesus dying on the cross during a sudden rainstorm as blood oozed from the spear wound of Jesus and was mixed with rainwater as it flowed down the side of the body. It was indeed an interesting interpretation, but it hardly represents what the evangelist was suggesting.)

The symbolic explanations are no less puzzling, but they may be a viable option for understanding the thinking process of the storyteller. Craig Koester links this concept of "blood and water" with John 6:53-55, where drink is linked with blood and bread with the flesh of Jesus, but the blood/drink symbolism does not fully handle the inclusion of water here.[167] Yet, some interpreters, including Koester, have speculated that the water could refer to baptism and be linked to John 3:5.[168] The combination, accordingly,

---

164 See G. Borchert, *John 12–21*, 274–75,

165 See P. Barber, *A Doctor at Calvary* (Garden City, NJ: Kennedy/Doubleday, 1953); D.A. Carson, *The Gospel According to John*, 623; and W. Edwards, et al., "On the Physical Death of Jesus," *Journal of the American Medical Association* 25.11 (1986): 1455–66.

166 A. Sava, "The Wounds of Christ," *CBQ* 19 (1957):242–46.

167 See Craig Koester, *Symbolism in the Fourth Gospel: Meaning, Mystery, Community* (Minneapolis: Fortress, 1995), 14, 181–84, 204, etc.

168 See G. Borchert, *John 1–11*, 270–72.

would then mean that blood and water refer to both baptism and the Lord's Supper/Eucharist, though in reverse order. But the order of "water and blood" does occur in the Johannine theological treatise that we call 1 John. There, "water and blood" are linked with the "Spirit" as the three witnesses that bear testimony to the coming of the "Son of God." This combination in 1 John 5:6-10[169] would strongly support a symbolic interpretation of water and blood as a reference to the two major sacred actions of the church—even though it leaves open the question of what, in fact, the Johannine witness to the event saw.

This crucifixion story then ends with a supporting purpose statement ("that you may believe," 19:35) that mirrors a portion of the main Johannine purpose statement in the gospel (20:30-31). It is then followed by what in contemporary literary studies would be a supporting double footnote (19:36-37) that confirms not a bone of the Passover Lamb shall be broken (Exod 12:46, Num 9:12) and acknowledges the prophecy that their king has been pierced (Zech 12:10).

The Burial of the King
(19:38-42)

The Death Story concludes with a brief reflection on the burial of Jesus. This narrative begins with Joseph of Arimathea, who has been a secret believer, requesting and being granted permission from Pilate to bury the body of Jesus (19:38).[170] He is joined in the burial process by Nicodemus, another secret believer, who first came to Jesus by night. Nicodemus supplies enough burial spices (a hundred Roman pounds) to bury a king. Together they take the body and, following the local pattern, they bind it with linen cloths and

---

169   See G. Borchert, *John 12–21*, 275. See also the discussion in Raymond Brown, *The Epistles of John, AB* (Garden City, NJ: Doubleday, 1982), 575–85.

170   According to Roman tradition dating back via Ulpian to Augustus, except in cases of treason (*maiestas*), the bodies of those executed by the state were to be released to the family or near friends if they were willing to bury them. It would be intriguing to know what Pilate was thinking in this case. See *The Digest of Justinian*, ed. T. Mommsen (Philadelphia: University of Pennsylvania Press, 1985), 48. 24. For comments, see, e.g., Raymond Brown, *The Death of the Messiah* (New York: Doubleday, 1994), 2. 1207.

spices and then place it in a new, unused, nearby garden tomb (19:39-41).[171] The evangelist ends this brief account with once again making sure that the reader knows that this event concludes on the day of Preparation—the day for sacrificing the Passover lambs!

While most stories about humans probably end at the point of their burial, with perhaps some additional comments concerning the legacy of those humans, that format hardly applies to the story of Jesus. His story certainly contains a long historical legacy that is contained in many books and will not be treated in this account, but his legacy is greatly dependent upon a different ending to his story than that of other people.

To that difference we now turn in the resurrection stories, but before doing so, the reader should pay special attention to the fact that there is no further mention of the haunting theme of Passover in John's gospel. The historic Passover is now over. It was a once-for-all-time event, although the wounds of Jesus will be evident to those early disciples who later see him as the risen Lord (20:20, 27). Accordingly, Jesus will forever remain the Lamb of God who takes away the sin of the world (1:29)!

Indeed, in the closing chapter of Revelation, the work penned by the Johannine Seer, Jesus remains the Lamb of God (Rev 22:3) who will be introduced not merely as the Lion King of Judah, the Root of David (Rev 5:5), but also as the slain yet standing, all-powerful, all-knowing Lamb of the future (5:6).

---

171 While I do not wish to enter into a discussion concerning the legitimacy of the Shroud of Turin, I would simply point out that this description of the burial of Jesus here (and of the burial wrappings of Lazarus) may not conform to what we know about the shroud. For a more traditional view, see R. Brown, *John*, 2.985. For further comments, see G. Borchert, *John 12–21*, 282, 294.

Chapter 7

The Primary Resurrection Stories
(20:1-29)

As I wrote years ago in an essay on the resurrection of Jesus, "All of the New Testament assumes the reality of the resurrection." There is no question that "for the New Testament writers," it is "the hinge point of Christianity."[172] Indeed, all those early writers would have agreed with Paul that "if Christ had not been raised, then my preaching is empty (*kenon*) and your faith is meaningless (*kene*)" (1 Cor 15:14). The Johannine evangelist would have totally rejected the non-material vision of Jesus and the removal of his body proposed by Joseph Klausner[173] and the mythologically conceived Easter Faith advocated by Rudolph Bultmann.[174]

My task here has not been an attempt to convince the committed rationalistic minds that Jesus was raised from the dead, but rather to communicate the Johannine story as well as I can and leave the task of convincing others to the Spirit of God.

While the Gospel of John may have apologetic features, it is first and foremost a testimony concerning the life, death, and resurrection of Jesus. The evangelist wrote his fascinating story to help people believe that Jesus is the Christ, the Son of God so that they might have new life through him (20:31). The gospel is not a documentary about Jesus, and the evangelist is not a newspaper reporter. From my perspective, he is a man who knew this Jesus, witnessed the resurrection of this Jesus, was transformed by this Jesus, became an evangelist for this Jesus, and wanted others to read his story about this Jesus. Therefore, I would want you to remember that this gospel is not a blow-by-blow account of the life of this Jesus. It is a purposeful collection of stories that assumes the resurrection of Jesus (please carefully read John 2:22 again). It was written many years after the resurrection. And I repeat that all

---

172 See Gerald L. Borchert, "The Resurrection: 1 Corinthians 15," *Review and Expositor* 80.3 (Summer 19883): 401.

173 Joseph Klausner, *Jesus of Nazareth* (London: George Allen & Unwin, 1925), 356–59.

174 Rudolph Bultmann, "New Testament Mythology" in *Kerygma and Myth*, ed. H. Bartsch (London: S.P.C.K.,1953), 339

these stories assume the resurrection. So let us now turn to the resurrection of this Jesus.

For convenience I have divided this chapter into three parts: the primary set of resurrection stories, the main purpose statement of the gospel, and the epilogue that was written after the main body of the gospel was completed. But I would add that I have found no evidence to suggest that the main segment ever circulated without this epilogue.

This primary set of resurrection stories is composed of four brief segments: the first discovery by Mary Magdalene, Peter, and the other disciple; the second discovery by Mary Magdalene; the transforming appearance to the disciples; and the Thomas story and the great confession.

The First Discovery:
Mary Magdalene, Peter, and the Other Disciple
(20:1-10)

In all four gospels women introduce the resurrection stories. In Mark (16:1) and Luke (24:1) they bring spices after the Sabbath to prepare the body of Jesus for his burial. In Matthew (28:1) the two Marys come early after the Sabbath to see the tomb. In John there is no mention of spices with the women because the King has already been prepared for burial. At this point in John, the evangelist reintroduces Mary Magdalene, who was only briefly mentioned earlier in this gospel as one of the women at the cross (John 19:25). And to conclude this general introduction, it is noteworthy to mention that all four gospels indicate that the day after Sabbath is when the women discover the empty tomb. It is the "first day of the week," and what has become the day of worship for Christians—not the Sabbath. It is the day of the resurrection!

In these resurrection accounts the Johannine storyteller continues his fascinating style of weaving multiple stories together to form a combined narrative. So, when we meet Mary Magdalene here,[175] she has come very early to the tomb and discovered that the stone which closed the tomb has been removed (20:1). Immediately, she changes her role from seeker in this gospel to that of messenger, running to tell the disciples—here primarily to both Peter and the disciple "whom Jesus loved"—about her discovery. Her message

---

175 For my comments on Mary Magdalene in the Gnostic gospels, see G. Borchert, *John 12–21*, 299.

is as succinct as a cablegram: "They have taken the Lord out of the tomb, and we do not know where they have laid him" (20:2). Her message is like the shout of "Fire!" for the disciples, and it receives prompt attention.

(I would remind you here of the idea that was promoted by the Jews at that time [cf. Matt 27:62-66, 28:11-15] and reasserted by Klausner and others that the disciples stole the body of Jesus and then pretended that he was raised from the dead. Such a theory would be too fantastic to believe unless you were predisposed to look for some reason to question the resurrection. The followers of Jesus were a beaten-up bunch and were hardly thinking of suggesting a pseudo-victory. They thought Jesus was dead and lying in a tomb.)

When those two disciples hear Mary's report, they rise to their feet quickly and begin a race to the tomb. (If the Beloved Disciple here is John, we would assume that he is much younger than Peter and easily outruns his older companion [20:3-4].) When the Beloved Disciple arrives at the tomb, he stops at the entrance and surveys the positioning of the burial wrappings. When Peter thereafter arrives, he rushes into the tomb and notes the burial cloths and particularly the way the head covering is rolled up and lying separated from the rest of the items (20:5-7).[176] The storyteller adds the following interesting comments as though he has personal information concerning that event: namely, that the other disciple entered, "saw and believed."[177] Yet at that point "they did not know the scripture" that indicated Jesus "must rise from the dead" (20:8-9). Finally, the two disciples return to their homes (20:10).

---

176 See my discussion of the grave wrappings above in G. Borchert, "The Burial of the King" and *John 12–21*, 282, 294.

177 One is tempted to ask: What did the Beloved Disciple believe at this point, and what is the significance of this notation? Hoskyns suggests that the "preeminence of the faith of the Beloved Disciple is the climax of the narrative." He also adds that "His faith was not derived from ancient prophetic texts; the fact of the empty tomb illuminated the sense of scripture," and he cites several texts—primarily Ps 16:10—to support his view. See E. Hoskyns, *The Fourth Gospel*, ed. N. Davey (London: Faber & Faber, 1956), 540. See also the discussion of the subordination of Peter in C.K. Barrett, *The Gospel According to St. John* (London: S.P.C.K., 1956), 468. See my earlier reference to this comparison between Peter and the Beloved/Other Disciple above and in G. Borchert, *John 12–21*, 293.

The Second Discovery: Mary Magdalene
(20:11-18)

As we pick up the story again, the scene has changed, and Mary is back visiting the tomb. There she sees a pair of sitting angels, one at the head and the other at the feet of where the body of Jesus had lain (20:11-12). When the angels ask "Why are you wailing?" she responds that "they have taken away my Lord" and she had no idea where they have put him (20:13).

Something very strange then happens. Someone is standing just behind her. She does not know who it is, but when she turns, she thinks he might be the gardener. In any case, he asks her the same question: "Why are you wailing?" Then he continues: "Who are you seeking?" Questions, questions, and more questions! But she responds with "If you have taken him away, just tell me ... I will go and get him" (20:14-15).

Note at this point that the Greek verb *klaiein* ("wailing"), which carries the sense of being in deep anguish, appears only eight times in this entire gospel: three times in the death story of Lazarus (11:31, 33, 33); once in the loneliness of the disciples when Jesus announces the coming of deep sorrow for them as he is about to die (16:20); and four times here in this deep sense of sorrow felt by Mary when she thinks that even the body of Jesus has been lost or stolen (20:11[two times], 13, 15)!

Then the stranger says just one more word: her name, "Mary!" It is as though a dark veil has fallen and she knows who it is: Jesus, her most revered teacher (*Rabboni*)! She just wants to grab him and never let him go![178] But he quickly tells her that she cannot hold on to him. She must let him go, because he will soon be ascending to the Father.

Mary obeys and Jesus gives her an important message to take to his follow- ers: "Tell them, I am ascending to my Father and their Father—to my God and their God!" Of course, Mary delivers the message to the disciples, saying, "I have seen the Lord and I am passing on his message to you!" (20:18).

In giving us these two brief discovery texts, the Johannine storyteller has provided us with a fascinating picture of two witnesses to the resurrection. The first is a man who believes because he saw the empty tomb. The second

---

178 The statement of Jesus that is often rendered as "Don't touch me," as in the KJV, is better translated in terms of "Don't hold on to me," as I have indicated above. It should not be viewed as if Jesus was a mere spirit and being unable to eat fish (Luke 24:42-43) or in opposition to the followers of Jesus being able to touch him (cf. Luke 24:39-40, John 20:27).

is a woman who believes because she experienced the appearance of the risen Lord. In the context of the ancient world where women's testimonies were often treated as suspect and where visions needed to be confirmed by factual physical evidence, this combined testimony is an amazing gift to the church that frequently demands a similar set of proofs—even today! But now it is time to turn to the resurrection appearance to the group of disciples

The Transforming Appearance to the Disciples
(20:19-23)

The day may have dawned for the Beloved Disciple and for Mary. It is for them the start of a new day for worship—the Lord's Day! It will soon foreshadow the arrival of the eschatological "Day of the Lord" that was predicted by the prophets (cf., e.g., Isa 2:11-19; 12:1, 6; Jer 31:6, 27-34; Ezek 34:11-12; Joel 2:1-2; Amos 5:18-20) and announced again in the New Testament in various texts (cf. John 39-40, 12:48; Matt 24:22, 36; 26:29; Rom 2:5, 16; Eph 4:30; 1 Thess 5:2-4; 2 Pet 3:10-11; Rev 6:16-17, 16:14; etc.)

Despite messages to the contrary, most of the disciples remain in darkness. It is the evening of the first day, and the disciples are assembled behind locked doors because of fear. Yet, a place with closed doors is not a problem for the risen Jesus. He surprisingly comes into their midst and suddenly stands among them. Then he greets them with the familiar Semitic greeting/blessing: "Peace be with you!" (20:19). But that is not all that happens. Jesus shows them his hands and side, leaving the disciples filled with joy when they see/recognize the Lord (20:20).[179] They are now witnesses to a resurrection Christophany (an appearance of the living Jesus).

(Those who have studied their Hebrew Bibles know that theophanies [appearances of God] do not usually happen without God giving the recipients a task or a commission. Would Jesus have a task for those who experienced his resurrection presence? I am sure you expect the answer will be in the affirmative.)

To conclude this memorable meeting of the disciples with the risen Lord, recall the elements of resources and the assignment the disciples receive on the evening of that first day of the new era with the risen Jesus:

---

179 The term "Lord" (*kurios*) used here was probably intended to have a divine lordship, although some scholars such as Haenchen consider it to be an editorial insertion. See Ernst Haenchen, *John 2* (Philadelphia: Fortress, 1984), 305.

- Jesus repeats his blessing of "Peace" upon them.
- Jesus commissions them to his mission, just as the Father has sent him.
- Jesus breathes on them and empowers them with the Holy Spirit,[180] much like God breathed on the first man, Adam, who became a "living being" (Gen 2:7).
- Jesus defines their task as the gracious ministry of bringing the message of the "forgiveness of sins to the world," and their failure to do so would be a damnable curse (20:21-23).[181]

This appearance and commission in John, therefore, should be considered as equivalent to the closing statement in the Gospel of Matthew where the risen Jesus not only appears to the disciples on a mountain in Galilee but also gives them a commission to go everywhere and proclaim the Good News and promises to be with them until the end of time (Matt 28:16-20)!

---

180 A number of scholars have been troubled by the fact that John here suggests that the giving of the Holy Spirit occurred at this point, whereas Luke in Acts 2:1-3 indicates that the Holy Spirit was given at Pentecost, fifty days later. To deal with this apparent conflict, B.F. Westcott (*The Gospel According to St. John* [Grand Rapids: Eerdmans, 1954], 2. 349–50) argued that the omission of the article before *pneuma hagion* meant that this event was preparatory to the actual giving of the Spirit. See also Beasley-Murray, *John*, 379–80. F.F. Bruce (*The Gospel of John* [Grand Rapids: Eerdmans, 1983], 392) rejects the particular argument, but still concludes with a two-stage argument by indicating that the Johannine text concerning the breathing relates to the empowerment for ministry. Don Carson (*The Gospel According to John* [Grand Rapids: Eerdmans, 1991], 651–55) adopts the old view of Theodore of Mopsuestia that the breathing represents the symbolic promise of the Holy Spirit being given. I realize that there are chronological problems when comparing John with the other gospels and Acts, but I do not think that chronology is a primary concern to the Johannine evangelist. I find these arguments typical of the Western mindset seeking to grapple with the Johannine use of time references.

181 I pause here briefly to indicate that the commission to forgive or to retain the sins of other humans has been debated by Christians for centuries. My basic sense of this controversial text is that Christians who are involved in "the forgiveness of sins" do so as their evangelistic commission to "win the world for Christ." They do so not as independent actors or contractors for God, but as agents of the Holy Spirit. Moreover, in this mission Christians function as members of the church, the Christian community, not as individuals. Accordingly, it is very difficult for me to agree with Raymond Brown who said, "the power to absolve and to hold men's sins is explicitly given to (ten of) the twelve in 20:23." See R. Brown, "The Kerygma of the Gospel According to John: The Johannine View of Jesus in Modern Studies," *Int* 21 (1967):39. See also Leon Morris, *The Gospel According to John*, NICNT (Grand Rapids: Eerdmans, 1995), 748–49. See my further comments in G. Borchert, *John 12–21*, 309–12.

The Thomas Story and the Great Confession
(John 20:24-29)

The final segment of the primary resurrection stories concludes with a focus on Thomas, the realist among the disciples. He misses that group's first meeting with Jesus on the first Lord's Day, but the other disciples inform him that they have seen the Lord. However, he makes a skeptic's firm pronouncement that unless he can verify the wounds of Jesus with his finger in the nail print and his hand in the spear hole, he will not believe (20:25).

Well, eight days later, which in Jewish reckoning of time means one week later—the next Lord's Day—Thomas makes sure he is at the disciples' meeting (20:26). Jesus also comes to their closed-door session! Again, Jesus begins by blessing them with "Peace."

I cannot help but imagine at that point what happened next. Jesus must have looked around the room, spotted Thomas, and said something like: "Hello, Thomas, I heard you said something after the last Lord's Day meeting." The throat of Thomas probably went completely dry. Then after Thomas had taken a deep breath, Jesus must have continued: "O.K., Thomas, come here and bring your finger!" "Yes," he did say. "Your finger." Then he undoubtedly added: "Bring your fist as well! Let's get this proof business out of the way, so you can be a believer" (20:27).

What comes next in the story is one of the most significant confessional statements in the entire New Testament. With all the passion of a skeptic-turned-believer, Thomas looks at Jesus and cries, "My Lord and my God!" (20:28)—words that would not come easy to a Jew, perhaps especially to the most realistic and questioning Jew among the disciples.

But then the evangelist adds a question and a conclusion to this Thomas story. The question of Jesus concerns Thomas' need to see in order to believe. (Is human seeing necessary for believing? I suppose that we in the twenty-first century still ask with the evangelist: What about us later skeptics who do not have the opportunity to see the risen Lord?) The answer of this resurrected, living Jesus is that he pronounces a divine blessing on those who have "not seen and yet believe" (20:29).

The storyteller must have known that the world is filled with skeptics, so he added the closing blessing to this thought-provoking story. Rudolf Schnackenburg points out that there is a fascinating parallel here with the Nathaniel story that concludes chapter 1 and the Cameos of Witness (1:44-51).

In both stories the skeptics after meeting Jesus offer significant confessions concerning their belief in Jesus.[182]

Thomas and Nathaniel are ideal models for many of us, who long to believe more convincingly in the resurrected Jesus but are sometimes filled with doubts and questions that periodically flash blinking red lights of doubt and skepticism. Although those doubts sometimes frustrate the tranquility of our faithfulness, God in the risen Christ continues to confirm us in our weak believing. And for that fact, we are exceedingly grateful.

In concluding these amazing confessions of both Nathaniel and Thomas, let us not forget that the disciples were strict monotheists who probably had grown up daily reciting the *shema*: "Hear, O Israel, the Lord our God, the Lord is one!" (Deut 6:4). Their understanding of God was likely very different than most humans in the Hellenistic world: they thought that God was so holy and remote that before they met Jesus, they may never have thought even to utter the *tetragrammaton* (*YHWH*), the name of God. Yet, Thomas expressed for all the disciples and for all succeeding generations of skeptics the confession that this Jesus truly possessed the attributes of Yahweh, the name of God in the Hebrew Bible. He probably thought: Could such claims that Jesus made throughout this gospel be possible?

In responding, remember that the disciples had witnessed Jesus getting tired in a boat and needing sleep, becoming thirsty and hungry while trekking through Samaria, and even needing to relieve himself. To confess then that this Jesus was both Lord and God took a revolution in their minds. The disciples may have been categorized as uneducated by the Jewish religious elite who regarded them to be among the *am haeretz* (the people of the land, laborers), but they were not stupid or uneducated (cf. Acts 4:13). Yet when they joined the company of Jesus, they were challenged in ways they had never countenanced. They were transformed!

The resurrection transformed these followers of Jesus into a mighty force that ultimately shook even the Roman empire, and it can shake us when we understand what the resurrection implies. It is not just a happy ending to a wrenching story, but as the purpose statement claims, it is the proclamation of power and life to those who believe.

---

182 R. Schnackenburg, *St. John*, 3.333.

Chapter 8

The Three Crucial Johannine Summarizing Texts
(20:30–21:25) (1:1-18)

The Pupose Statement of the Gospel (20:30-31)

The first draft of this fascinating gospel most likely ended with the force-ful two-verse purpose statement in which the evangelist attempted to bring together many of the themes he had introduced previously. The result is a brilliant summation that is both very comprehensive and at the same time exceedingly precise. Like many other parts of this gospel, it is a literary jewel.

It begins with an acknowledgement that this storybook could have included more "signs" that Jesus did in the presence of his disciples, suggesting both revelational and educational elements in the actions and teachings of Jesus. But the use of the term "signs" in this statement has created some serious debate among scholars because the entire gospel does not necessarily fit the usual meaning of special revelational acts or actions on the part of Jesus. The result is that some like Robert Fortna have sought to find an early "signs source" lurking within the gospel.[183] But such a quest, I suggest, while it may be interesting, is hardly a meaningful tangent to take.

Instead, I prefer to join the evangelist as he focuses on the reason for his selection of the details. The purpose of this statement is nothing less than to bring about believing in Jesus who is the main character or the subject of this gospel. In pursuit of this goal, the Johannine storyteller seems to be proposing a change in the way one addresses Jesus because believing seems to be focused on the role that the resurrected Jesus plays in the believing community: namely, he is for the community none other than Jesus, the Christ (Messiah), or Jesus, the Son of God (20:31).

When one examines the first Johannine epistle, one notices the intriguing fact that Jesus is no longer addressed there simply as Jesus but either as Jesus Christ/Jesus, the Christ or as Jesus, the Son of God. I suggest, therefore, that

---

183 For Fortna's extended discussion on a signs source, see *The Fourth Gospel and Its Predecessor* (Philadelphia: Fortress, 1988). For my further comments on signs, see G. Borchert, *John 1–11*, 42–50.

the thinking in this purpose statement has either mirrored or influenced the thinking in 1 John. In that tightly argued theological treatise, the one "who denies that Jesus is the Christ" is nothing but a "liar" and has the spirit of "the antichrist" (1 John 2:22). But confessing both that "Jesus Christ has come in the flesh is of God" (4:3) and that "Jesus is the Son of God" means that "God abides in that one" (4:15).

Names were very important to the descendants of Abraham because names were precious and were identified with the nature of the person. To believe in one's name implied that the name is a reliable expression of who the person is (John 2:23). So, to ask in one's name signified trust in the power of that one to deliver the request (14:13, 14; 16:24, 26). Also, to be kept by a name meant to be secure in that person (17:11, 12).

The name of Jesus was very crucial to this storyteller and to the purpose statement of this gospel. Believing in his name or in the saving nature of Jesus is therefore linked directly to the evangelist's understanding of having or receiving new life—the foundational reason of why the prologue informs us that the divine word became flesh/human and dwelt/tented among humans (1:14).

For John, believing could never be understood as a mere acceptance of a creedal formulation. That is the primary reason why the evangelist completely avoided using the nouns for "faith" (*pistis*) and "knowledge" (*gnōsis*), and instead used only the verbs such as *pisteuein* ("believing") *ginōskein* and *oida* ("knowing"). For this storyteller, what you believe and what you know would always be subordinated to who you know and in whom you believe. It is a crucial strategy: every time he used those verbs rather than the nouns, it emphasized a living relationship with a dynamic God.

When Loisy reached the final stage in writing his commentary on John, he declared in his memorable statement: *"Le Livere est fini, tres bien fini!"*[184] While his words can easily be translated into English, they hardly will be rendered in the flourish of the French original. While I differ in what Loisy meant by his historic statement, I agree that the Johannine evangelist wove a magnificent storybook tapestry in this work known as the Gospel of John. It is a masterpiece of storytelling and at the same time a brilliant example of theological reflection. But when the evangelist had completed his initial manuscript (twenty chapters), he must have quickly realized that his work required a few additional words.

---

184 A. Loisy, *Le quatrieme evangile* (Paris: Emile Nourrey, 1921), 514. "The book is finished very well completed!"

He really had not given sufficient attention to the way his model storybook had begun. It was a magnificent document, but it needed a much better introduction. And he determined that he would supply it. To that introduction, which we call the prologue, I will turn after I complete the epilogue.

Yes, the manuscript also needed an epilogue to deal with two important concerns: the continuing status of Peter and the issue of the long life of the community's Beloved Disciple. Denying Jesus was a serious issue. The evangelist was not concerned with the devil-man, Judas. He had long ago been confirmed as a traitor and had vanished from the scene, but that was not true of Peter. The Johannine community needed to know that Peter had been restored by Jesus, that he had suffered as an authentic martyr, and that his memory needed to be affirmed throughout the extended Christian community. But the Christian world also needed to know that their Beloved Disciple was truly human and that, even though he was now very old, Jesus did not say he would not die. So, to these concerns we now turn our attention.

The Epilogue (21:1-25)

As I indicated earlier, the draft of this fascinating storybook that we call John was originally completed at the end of chapter 20, but it needed a better beginning (a prologue) and an extended ending (epilogue) to deal with a couple of issues that were not treated. Scholars naturally have had various opinions about this concluding segment of the gospel—all the way from rejecting it as a composite editorial addition[185] to a later addition by the same author. The most common opinion with various adjustments is that an ecclesiastical redactor added the segment.[186] Boismard, however, proposed the rather novel idea that the epilogue was the work of Luke. But that view has had little acceptance because it hardly represents Luke's style.[187]

After reviewing the various proposals, I still consider the earlier thesis of B.F. Westcott to be the most likely, namely that the addition was added by the same author. Westcott contends that there is no evidence that the gospel

---

185 See R.H. Smith, *Easter Gospels* (Minneapolis: Augsburg,1983), 171–76.
186 See Beasley-Murray, *John*, 395–95; Bultmann, *John*, 700–701; R. Brown, *John*, 2.1080; Schnackenburg, *St. John*, 3. 341–45.
187 M. Boismard, *"le chapitre xxi de saint Jean: essai de critique literaire,"* RB 54 (1947), 473–501.

ever circulated without the addition.[188] Moreover, E. Ruckstuhl has also convincingly shown that linguistically and stylistically there are few grounds for arguing that chapter 21 was written by anyone other than the author of the rest of the gospel.[189]

Concerning the organization of this chapter, I believe it naturally breaks into three segments: the appearance to the seven while fishing, the fireside discussion with Peter, and the authentication and conclusion.

The Appearance to the Seven at the Sea (21:1-8)

Chapter 21 begins with the vague Greek expression *meta tauta* ("after these things"), which provides no assistance concerning the chronological context except to note that the evangelist informs us later that this story represents "the third time" that Jesus appeared to the disciples following his resurrection (21:14).[190] Then returning to the first verse, it says Jesus "showed/revealed" (*ephanerōsen*) himself to the disciples. The verb is quite general and does not necessarily mean a resurrection appearance, but we soon learn that the event took place by the Sea of Tiberias, otherwise known as the Sea of Galilee.

Then seven disciples, who are noted here, are said to have gone fishing. Several commentors have suggested that the text implies that these disciples were abandoning their relationship with Jesus. Brown even posits that they were entering "aimless activity in desperation." Beasley-Murray counters by asking "how the learned professor knows" this fact since there is no "hint of aimlessness" or "desperation" in the text. But I have also noted that Beasley-Murray then adds his rationale for the fishing that "the disciples must still *eat*." Of course, in this post-Schweitzer era, psychoanalyzing Jesus from a story about Jesus is now regarded as completely illegitimate because we cannot do such an analysis from a story about someone else. Nevertheless, everyone likes

---

188 See B.F. Westcott, *The Gospel According to St. John* (Grand Rapids: Eerdmans, 1954), 2. 359–60.

189 See E Ruckstuhl, *Die literarische Einheit des Johannesevangeliums* (Freiburg: Paulus, 1951) and G. Borchert, *John 12–21*, 320–21.

190 For my brief discussion on the thorny issue of places and when the resurrection appearances took place, which was raised by Lohmeyer, see my Excursus "Jerusalem and Galilee" in G. Borchert, *John 12–21*, 323–24.

to construct his or her stories about Jesus using speculation.[191] Yet, great care needs to be exercised in storytelling!

Now, when the disciples of Jesus are usually mentioned as a group, the number twelve normally comes to mind, but here the number given is seven. Both numbers are significant in biblical thinking, as they have a sense of completeness and are formed from different combinations of three and four—the usual basic numbers reflecting matters pertaining to the divine and the world orders. Of the seven persons mentioned here, Peter (1) and Thomas (2) are included in the synoptic lists, Nathaniel (3) is not mentioned in the Synoptics, but is popularly thought to be Bartholomew (yet he is not otherwise so identified); the two sons of thunder (4 and 5), James and John, are next mentioned, but they are not elsewhere so identified in this gospel (this note is crucial when thinking of who the evangelist might be); and finally, two unidentified disciples are also noted in this list (6 and 7).[192]

This story is reminiscent of the similar story in Luke 5:1-11 where early in his ministry Jesus called the disciples to fish for people. Naturally, the similarity between the stories in Luke and John has led scholars to argue that one or other of the stories is a misplaced pericope. (To enter a comparison of the two stories here would extend this work considerably and involve several excurses related to chronology, geography, harmonization, and the nature of appearances in Jerusalem and Galilee—which was the focus of one of my earlier theses and that is beyond the scope of this work. Accordingly, my goal here is to concentrate on this fishing story itself before moving to the more significant issue of the restoration of Peter.)

The actual story begins with Peter announcing that he is going fishing (21:3). The others agree to join him in the experience. All that night their efforts prove fruitless and produce nothing. As dawn is breaking, someone on the shore calls to them and asks if they have caught anything. When they respond in the negative, the man on the shore tells them to throw their net on the right side of the boat and they will be successful (21:5).

(Now it might sound a bit crazy for seasoned fishermen to follow advice from someone on the land, especially after a fruitless night of work. But, as J.A. Bernard points out, perhaps Jesus saw a shoal of fish on the right side of

191 See R. Brown, *John*, 2.1096. See then Beasley-Murray, *John*, 399. Thereafter see G. Borchert, *John 12–21*, 325–326.
192 The lists can be found in Mark 3:11-19, Matt 10:1-4, Luke 6:12-16, and Acts 1:13.

the boat.[193] That suggestion is an attempt to make silence speak to the rational mind or to imply that there was something supernatural about the stranger on the shore. In either case, it is probably best to let silence remain silence.)

Well, the disciples follow the stranger's suggestion, and the net is loaded with fish (21:6)—a weird sight for them, no doubt. Then the Beloved disciple recognizes Jesus: "It is the Lord!" and he delivers the news to Peter. When Peter hears the report, he puts on his clothing (he had been stripped: *gumnos/gymnos* = "naked") and jumps into the lake to get to Jesus quickly.[194] They are only a short distance from land at that point, so the rest of the group comes ashore dragging the net full of fish (21:8).

The Fireside Discussion with Peter (21:9-23)

When the disciples all arrive on shore, they meet with a strange scene. It is a friendly fire with fish and bread, but yet a bit strange. It is a charcoal fire (*anthrakian*), which undoubtedly raises a haunting memory for at least one person in the group (21:9; cf.18:18). But Jesus says to bring some fish. So, Peter goes back to the boat and hauls the net with fish ashore. And they even count the fish—153 (21:11).

(The brevity of the account concerning Peter's arrival and the handling of the fish has given rise to scores of questions and thus to debates among scholars concerning the meaning of statements in the text and to suggestions of possible editing of the account. Jerome, in commenting on the text of Ezekiel 47 where the stream from the temple brings life to the Dead Sea [Ezek 47:9-10], relied on the zoologist Oppianus Coilex to indicate there would be 153 species of fish there.[195] Augustine also tried his hand at interpreting the number of 153 and thought that the significance lay in the sum of the numbers of 1 to 17.[196] I have suggested other possibilities. But what can be said is that it was a good haul of fish that morning! Yet these matters are only the framework for what is

---

193 J.A. Bernard, *A Critical and Exegetical Commentary on the Gospel of According to St. John*, ICC (Edinburgh: T&T Clark, 1928), 2. 696.

194 C.K. Barrett (*The Gospel According to St. John* [London: S.P.C.K., 1956], 482) reminds us that, according to tradition, the religious did not pass greetings to each other without being clothed.

195 See Jerome, *Commentary on Ezekiel in Migne, PL*, 25. 474c. Actually, Oppianus argued for the number of 157.

196 See Augustine's reflections on John in section 122.8 (Migne, *PL*, 35.1963–64).

the very important conversation between Jesus and Peter. And to that discussion I now turn.)

When they have completed their breakfast, Jesus addresses Peter three times in a very formal manner: "Simon, son of John, do you love me [more than these]?" (21:15 *agapas*, 21:16 *agapas*, and 21:17 *phileis*). Peter responds three times, but with slight variations: "Yes, Lord, you know that I love you" (21:15 *philō*, 21:16 *philō*, 21:17 *philō*). Many interpreters focus on the fact that there are two Greek words for "love" used in these threefold questions, noting that the third time Jesus changes the verb from *agapas* to *phileis*. Some scholars then suppose that Jesus may have come down to the meaning of love with Peter.

Now there may be some hint that Jesus may have moved a little in this discussion on love, as the evangelist did change his use of the Greek verb. But as I have said many times to my students, "A little knowledge of Greek can be dangerous." There are unanswered questions: Would Jesus have been talking to Peter in Greek or Aramaic-Hebrew? Did the storytelling evangelist think there was a significant difference between the two verbs for "love" that are used here? This question is not a mere academic one: If you check John 5:20, you will discover that the evangelist says "the Father loves the Son" and that the Greek verb there is *philei*. Does this mean that the Father's love for the Son is a subordinate love? I would remind you that the text itself tells you why Peter was grieved, and it was not because of the change of verbs! It was because Jesus asked him "a third time"—"Do you love me?" (21:17). But the conversation is even more intriguing.

When Jesus responds three times to Peter after the disciple answers that he loves Jesus, the subsequent response of Jesus is very interesting. In each of the three responses, Jesus gives Peter a crucial charge or a commission: "Feed (*boske*) my lambs" (21:15); Tend (*poimaine*) my sheep" (21:16); and "Feed (*boske*) my sheep" (21:17). A charge that is given three times is not intended to be changed.

(The haunting memory of his denial probably never left Peter's memory, and the storyteller may well have known such to be the case. The reason I make this statement is that when you check the epistle that is attributed to Peter, you will discover that in his advice to younger elders, the Petrine writer advises the elders: "Tend [*poimanate*] the flock which God has placed in your charge" [1 Pet 5:2]. Peter's charge in that first epistle is not simply coincidental. Those statements are clearly related. I think it was part of the church's stark memory that took place in a fireside discussion many years before [cf. the NLT Version's rendering of Paul's advice to the Ephesian elders in Acts 20:28]).

But having issued his threefold charge to Peter, it is now time to address the future of both Peter and the other disciples. In the solemnity of this discussion and with Peter's earlier offer to "lay down his life for Jesus" as a background (John 13:37), Jesus must have looked directly at Peter and with another double *amēn* oath-like statement said to his dear servant, "When you are old, you are going to be taken into custody and you are going to 'stretch out your hands,' then die the death of a martyr" (21:18-19). Hard words? Yes, indeed! Was Peter ready for them? I doubt it! Peter tries to shift the subject to a comparison with the Beloved Disciple who is there.

That shift is a tailor-made opening for the evangelist to deal with another important issue. Rumors and theories are floating around the Johannine community concerning their elder hero. The gossip is that Jesus predicted that the Beloved Disciple will live until Jesus returns. The leaders know that such gossip is a misunderstanding of what Jesus told Peter: Peter's concern is to follow Jesus! Like Peter, the Johannine community is getting the wrong focus on their hero. Like the early Christians, we later followers of Jesus need to understand that a misunderstood focus on an issue can be a recipe for problems among us, just as it was for the early church.

The Authentication and Conclusion (21:24-25)

John's epilogue and the need for an authentication provides another stark reminder that the Christian community was faced with people who mis-represented Jesus and his teachings. Indeed, the Johannine epistles provide clear evidence that there were liars who denied that Jesus was the Christ and/or that he was the Son of God (1 John 2:22-23). By now we should also be aware that these two confessions were crucial confessions to the Johannine evangelist because they were central to his purpose statement of humans experiencing new life in the name of Jesus (John 20:31). Thus, the heroic elder John, in writing his theological treatise (1 John) regarded people who deny these confessions as having the spirit of antichrist (3:2-3).

Today, in our American pseudo-polite society, we may regard people who make such defining statements as narrow or out of touch with contemporary mores. But when we understand that evil does not actually have a polite or accepting countenance and that Christians in fact did and do die for their faith, then clarity of one's confession was and is essential. Protecting the transmission of the gospel messages was a major necessity because people did not hesitate to misrepresent themselves as authentic Christians and were quite ready to alter the meaning of what true proclaimers of the gospel said. That is the reason methods of authentication had to be developed, as is indicated in John 21:24.

Even in the time of the early epistles, the Apostle Paul developed his own patterns for authenticating his manuscripts by taking the pen from his *amanuensis* (scribe) and marking his letters with his personal certification (see, e.g., 1 Cor 16:21, Gal 6:11, Eph 6:21, Col 4:18, 2 Thess 3:17, and Phlm 19). Similarly, in the closing verses of John's gospel the church elders added their protective authentication.

Then before or after the authentication was installed, the storyteller brought this fascinating storybook to a grand conclusion by suggesting that what Jesus had accomplished during his brief life in the world was so extensive that recording all the details would be such an immense task that the world could hardly hold the books that would be written about him (John 21:25). (Of course, this statement draws a friendly smile from readers who enjoy creative overstatements. And such has occurred in my family when my son, Mark—also a professor—delights in teasing me that I have written several shelves of books in seeking to fulfill the evangelist's prediction.) Seriously, the evangelist's closing statement is an appropriate value reflection concerning the most important person who ever lived, namely, the one the prologue identifies as the divine "Word who became flesh and tented" in our midst for a few short years (1:14) and is the unique Lamb of God who takes away the sin of the world (1:29). And so, it is time to address the prologue.

The Encompassing Prologue (1:1-18)

In concluding this storybook interpretation, I turn to closing this magnificent story of Jesus by reflecting on the marvelous prologue after the rest of the gospel was finished. I repeat that I have no textual or other hard evidence to support my theory that the prologue was finished last. But as Westcott argued concerning the later addition of the epilogue to the gospel by the same author,[197] I think the prologue was written as an introductory summation by the same author after the storybook sections were completed. The gospel was never circulated without the prologue.

The prologue (1:1-18) begins the gospel with one of the most elevated statements of Christology in the New Testament, rivaled perhaps only by statements from Paul in Colossians (Col 1:15-20), by the Preacher of Hebrews in his introduction (Heb 1:1-13), and by the Johannine Apocalyptic Dreamer in his threefold opening statement and startling vision of Christ (Rev 1:1-20).[198]

The structure and nature of these first eighteen verses in the Gospel of John are brilliantly designed as though they were developed by an artistic writer. The poetic reality of this prologue has led scholars to posit various patterns for understanding the format, including suggestions that it is a poem (J.T. Sanders), a hymn in four strophes (Raymond Brown), an Aramaic hymn (C.F. Burney), a clever chiastic statement (Alan Culpepper), and a poem in the style of a Jewish wisdom hymn (Ben Witherington).[199]

Among the notable features of this hymn/poem is the fact that there is implied a community making the affirmations or statements here (see the "we" and "us" in 1:14 and 1:16), which are confirmed by the community's authentication of this work in the epilogue (21:24) and implied by the community's acceptance of the Johannine witness (19:35).

---

197 B.F. Westcott, *The Gospel According to St. John* (Grand Rapids: Eerdmans, 1954), 2.359–60.

198 For my comments on these texts, see Gerald L Borchert, *Portraits of Jesus for an Age of Biblical Illiteracy* (Macon, GA: Smyth & Helwys, 2016), 46, 97, 133–34, 161–62.

199 J.T. Sanders, *The New Testament Christological Hymns: Their Historical Religious Background* (Cambridge: University Press, 1971), 20–24; R. Brown, *John*, 1. 3–5; C.F. Burney, *The Aramaic Origin of the Fourth Gospel* (Oxford: Clarendon, 1922), 40; R.A. Culpepper, "Pivot of John's Prologue," NTS 27 (1980): 17; B. Witherington III, *John's Wisdom* (Louisville: Westminster John Knox, 1995), 47–48. See my more extended discussion with footnote in G. Borchert, *John 1–11*, 160–62.

While it would take many pages to unfold the full importance of the ideas that are packed in these eighteen verses, my goal here is to provide a brief summary or overview of how this prologue introduces the most unique person to enter human history and why the stories that follow are so significant. A crucial feature of this poetic introduction is the way it demonstrates how to read the stories of Jesus in relation to the Father: even though a high Christology is asserted here, there is no attempt to displace the priority of God (the Father). Here, clearly asserted is the fact that the "Word/Person" is "from the beginning" (1:1) and is identified to be God (*theos*, 1:1). Moreover, he has been and is fully active in the creation of all things (1:2), possesses life in himself (1:4), is the source of light and enlightenment for humanity (1:4), shines into the darkness with unquenchable force (1:5), and therefore is equated with God.

Yet this "Word/Person," who is identified as God, must also be distinguished from God (*pros ton theon*, 1:1), and he takes his cues from God—the Father (1:14, 18).

Equally significant is the fact that although this "Word/Person" was involved in creating the world, he was strangely unknown in it (*kosmos/idia*, 1:10-11), and he was rejected by the world and even by his own historic people (*idioi*, 1:11). Nevertheless, he was declared to be in the bosom (*eis ton kolpon*) of the Father.[200] What an amazing summation concerning this "Word/Person." It is almost as though the Johannine storyteller was attempting to retain the belief in monotheism and yet to assert a multi-dimensional understanding of God. I am convinced that such a strategy was his goal.

Closely related to the above statement, the storyteller seems to be attempting to explain the incarnation by his use of two Greek verbs. When he deals with issues related to the eternal nature of God, he uses the verb *eimi* ("is" or "was"). But when he deals with the earthly reality, he uses the verb *ginomai* ("become" or "come to be"). Thus, when he wanted to insert John the Baptizer into the discussion here and thereby connect this prologue with the rest of the storybook (the gospel), he used *ginomai*, but English translations find it hard to indicate this difference and usually render the statement as "There was a man" (*egeneto*, 1:6). Fortunately, when the discussion concerns Jesus moving from the eternal realm to our realm of time and space, then English

---

200   Note that in the story part of the gospel, one of his followers, the Beloved Disciple, was seen to be lying in the breast of or next to (*en tō kolpō*) Jesus at the triclinium meal on the night Jesus was betrayed by another follower (1:18; cf. 13:25).

versions adequately render the statement as "And the Word became flesh" (human=*egeneto*, 1:14).

But there is more in this magnificent poetic statement, and it involves dealing with those who were created by this "Word/Person." God's plan was not simply that this "Word/Person" should become (*egeneto*) human but that all those who received him should gain the powerful authority "to become" (*genesthai*) the children of God (1:12). How would they become children of God? Do you remember the purpose statement of John? Well, the crucial part of that purpose statement is included in this prologue. Those humans who "believe in his name" (*tois pisteuousin eis ta onoma autou*, 1:12; cf. 20:31) are the ones who will become the children of God.

I have taken the time to explain the use of a few Greek words here to help readers understand how skillful the evangelist was in crafting this prologue. Indeed, as we continue to read John 1:14, the King James translators correctly, I believe, picked up a fascinating pictorial wordplay of the Greek verb *eskēnōsen*. They rendered the evangelist's verb as Jesus, the Word "tabernacled" or "tented" among humans rather than using the common English word "dwelt" as is used by the translators of the RSV and other versions.

I believe that Cyrus Gordon (the famed linguist at Brandeis University who developed the theory of the bridge between Semitic and Minoan cultures) would have been delighted here in the possibility of reducing the Greek verb *skēnoun* into the basic Semitic three consonantal stem of *SKN*, which fascinatingly is the root for the Hebrew noun *shikinah*. The *shekinah* was pictured by Israel as "God's presence with them"[201] in the tabernacle or tent of meeting, which was the setting where the glory of the Lord was said to reside (see, e.g., Exod 40:34-38, Lev 9:23, Num 14:10). So, with this thought in mind and to draw the evangelist's picture-thinking to a conclusion, let me suggest that it was not a big step for the storyteller—who had been steeped in the faith of Israel—to confess with the Johannine community concerning

---

201 For a discussion of the "*skēnē*" family, see W. Michaelis, *TDNT* 7.368–94. For a different view, see J.C. Merger, "John 1:14 and the New Temple," *JBL* 88 (1969):57–68.

Jesus: "We have seen his glory, the glory of the one and only Son[202] from the Father (1:14).[203]

After this important confession, the evangelist then parenthetically ties his important affirmations to the story of the Baptizer that will follow this prologue. He begins by introducing the theme of the Baptizer's unworthiness before he reminds us that we all (everyone) have (has) "received grace against grace" (super-abundant grace, 1:16). In doing so, he places Jesus (the Word) in his well-known Jewish historical context by reminding the reader that the law was a gift of God's earlier grace but that the law has now been superseded by the incarnation of God's Son, Jesus Christ.

Then returning to his earlier mention of "fullness," the evangelist proclaims that the "fullness" of grace and truth was given not through Moses but through Jesus, the Christ—the only one who had fulfilled the purposes of God. This Jesus is the only one who has seen God (1:18). Thus, because he came from God, he is capable of making God known to humanity (1:17-18). What a fascinating way to set the stage for highlighting the main person (character) in the Gospel of John—the work that I consider to be the model of storytelling about Jesus the Christ, the Son of God. If you believe in him, he offers you the opportunity for new life with God (cf. 20:31)!

Do you not agree that this prologue is a magnificent summary of God's purpose in sending Jesus into the world and also a superb introduction to the model stories about his brief time as an incarnated human on Planet Earth?

---

202 I find the NIV translation of monogenous in our current multi-religious generation to be attractive as compared to the usual "only begotten" because it eliminates any possibility of arguing that there were other Sons of God.
203 See my extended discussion on this pictorial statement in G. Borchert, *John 1–11*, 118–123.

A Brief Postscript

As we reach the conclusion to our brief time together, I trust you have begun to understand a little of why the Gospel of John keeps calling me back to its pages. I cannot get away from its intriguing stories and its haunting themes. But in closing, I should tell you a little more of my story. Years ago, when I was boy in grade school, I was taken by ambulance to a hospital in Calgary, Alberta, and told I would be in isolation for about a month. Before I left, my brother, Don, stuck a small paperback copy of the New Testament in my hand: the Gospel of John became my companion.

When I left the hospital, I returned home with most of this gospel memorized. John's words have been with me when I taught that gospel on TV (with one of my former students[204]) for the *Chicago Sunday Evening Club*, in Israel (as I described in the Introduction to this work), and in many schools—including in at least a dozen other countries around the world. And even though I have written several thousand pages on this gospel that contains a mere 21 chapters, I have not exhausted the new insights that keep coming to me. The Gospel of John is, indeed, an inspiring work. And like other sections of our biblical canon, it can draw humans into the presence of God where its words and stories become models for relationships, keys to behavior, patterns for thought, and directives for life.

My prayer for you, therefore, is that the words of John and of our beloved Scriptures will dwell in you as God's highway to your genuine authenticity.

---

204 Manfred Brauch later became the president of Palmer Seminary in Philadelphia.

Selected General Index

*References to acts and works by Gerald L. Borchert are not included.

CPSIA information can be obtained
at www.ICGtesting.com
Printed in the USA
JSHW052119220523
41995JS00007B/25